My Proclamation

By R. B. Barms

Because the father deserves no respect, he is referred to as "he" – not even capitalized at the beginning of the sentence.

ISBN: 978-1-62249-524-5

Published by
The Educational Publisher Inc.
Biblio Publishing
Columbus, Ohio
BiblioPublishing.com

The Beginning

There are certain things a child should be provided to have a nice life. These are very basic things: a home that is safe, food and water, education, and love. Up until the age of 9, I was pretty lucky to have these basic things provided to me, plus, I was given a pretty nice life with all the extras that I could have asked for. I was able to have nice clothes, the ability to play any sport I wanted, and had most things within reason that I asked for. My stomach was never hungry, I was provided with the best education, and my mom provided me with more love than I could have ever asked for.

During these first 9 years there was only one thing missing. When most people think of a family, they think of a mom and dad, a couple kids and maybe a cat or dog. Where I was blessed with the best mom anyone could ever ask for, I was also cursed with the worst human being as my father. This man terrorized my life and the lives of the rest of my family for as long as I can remember.

People used to believe that they could remember memories back to the age of three. Now it is believed that because of child amnesia, the real age is seven. Because of my young age, amnesia has not set in yet. I can remember things back to the age of three and I have zero good memories of *him*. What I am left with is nightmares, panic attacks, anxiety, and my basic needs taken away. I am left with fear, exhaustion, and always the unknown. I am left with anger, a reason to fight, and a need to have my voice heard. I am left with only words.

When I was around the age of three, my family lived in an old farmhouse in Central Ohio. It was surrounded by cornfields and other farms. The house was small and smelled strange. The walls were covered with the same exact materials as the floors. During the summer months it had the biggest spiders you could ever imagine. The only thing I really liked about this house was the play set that was there. It had a couple swings and a spiral slide. My older sister and I played there often. *he* wasn't home a lot during these days. That has always been the only positive where *he* is concerned. We lived very close to the zoo so we frequented it often. My mom was able to buy us season passes, so it was a nice get-away for a couple hours here and there. Occasionally, we were able to ride the rides, which was a blast.

For some reason this day *he* decided to tag along. I don't remember much about the actual day at the zoo. I am uncertain if *he* screamed at us in an unusual way or if *he* decided to call us names, because apparently ours were not good enough. I do not recall if *he* refused to let us be actual kids - the behavior *he* hated the most. The memory that sticks into my head is the one that happened afterwards when we stopped for dinner. I remember the restaurant kind of being like our house. It must have been an older and not popular place. I also remember that there were only a few people inside. My little sister Scarlett was only one at the time and was still breastfeeding. She had been crying before we arrived because it was time for her to eat.

When we sat down at the tables, we ordered our food and my mom started to feed Maci. It wasn't until the food came that Elaina and I finally had to go to the bathroom. I don't know why our bodies work that way. Why we always have to go at the worst times. My mom, who was occupied at the time, asked *him* if he could take us. *he* has always been a big jerk when it comes to *his* food. *he* always has to eat first, *he* will not share *his* food, and *he* refuses to eat it cold. *he* was not happy with my mom for asking *him* to be an actual parent. *he* responded with a comment calling us bastards. At the age of eleven I am still not 100% certain on what that word means. I could Google it and it would click in my brain, but you can imagine what a three-year-old would like about that. I didn't understand what that word meant, but for years I thought I was one.

There are a few things that drive my mom crazy. She is really weird about how we carry scissors, how we act around a fire pit, and we are not allowed to climb up slides. Even if I do it now at the age eleven, she is going to tell me we can leave the park. While living at the Our first house I really only have one other memory. Elaina (my older sister), my cousins, and I were playing on our play set. My grandpa, *his* dad, brought them up, and he was hanging out with

My Proclamation

my mom. This was back when they were still nice to her. We had been playing kind of like a chase game or maybe tag around the play set. Elaina had talked me into climbing up the slide to try to tag her. I had almost reached the very top when she decided to come down. Her body weight shifted, and the way I was standing caused me to flip off the side. I landed hard onto my hand. I remember the pain and Elaina's laugh. I started screaming because the pain was unbearable. My mom came running over to grab me. One look at my wrist and she told my grandpa that she was going to take me to the emergency room. After Elaina heard how bad it really was, her cackles turned to sobs. I still, to this day, think she meant to do it. Not making me fall off the side of the slide because who can think that up as a little kid, but I think she meant to cause me to fall down the slide.

The ER doctors were all very nice. I was given a red popsicle and some juice. It turned out that I broke my wrist and was given a purple cast that I was going to have to wear for many weeks. I had to take a long break from doing gymnastics. I was very sad about this because my best friend, Scarlett, was there. Her dad was an Ohio State University football coach. Her mom, Katie, was a very good friend of my mom's. She would later visit at our next house, come to Jack's birthday party, and take my mom to a Nebraska game with her. I always really liked the Cox family.

The summer when I was four, is the summer we moved into my house. Even though I no longer reside there, I still consider it my home. This house would come to be my sanctuary and my hell. Most of my memories exist in this house. Coming from the small house in Our first house, the Dovetail house seemed like a mansion. It had four bedrooms and we could use them all. It did not smell strange and the walls actually had paint on them. We had a really big yard and neighbors who we could, and did become friends with. It was right across the street from the elementary school where I would attend. The teachers' parking lot would be where my mom taught all four of us how to ride our bikes, where we would ride our scooters and have races. We spent countless hours doing both. The playground was where we would meet our friends, hit baseballs, play basketball, and play ground beef.

As I type about this house, it causes me to almost cry because I still really miss living there. I miss jumping on my trampoline, playing on

3

our gigantic water slide, riding our bikes to our friend's house, I just miss it all. Everyone knew the Barms lived there. It would become a hangout for adults and kids up until we had to leave.

Peanuts and peanut butter are such important and popular food items that I do not understand how Scarlett escaped touching them or coming into contact with them for two years. My mom used to buy a bag of peanuts with the shells on them, and we would eat them - we meaning everyone else because Scarlett was still little. It was right after we moved in that my mom decided to introduce us to peanut butter and jelly sandwiches. None of us liked them and still do not to this day, but my mom wouldn't know that at the time. By this time my brother, Jack, was born. We moved into this house when he was maybe six months old. My mom had made the sandwiches and then sat down on the floor by the kitchen to play with Jack. Maybe a couple minutes went by when Scarlett went to my mom and kinda moaned about her face hurting. My mom took one look at her and jumped up. You know how I said that the positive thing about *him* was that he was never home. It carried on to this house, too. My mom had started becoming good friends with our next door neighbors. They would live there for a couple years before they would build a huge house on a golf course in Delaware.

The Reed's had tons of doctors in their family so my mom rushed Scarlett over to Karrie's house to see if it was what she thought it was. She also asked Karrie to watch the three of us so she could take Scarlett to the ER. Karrie had two kids, Charlie and Dawson. They were Mine and Jack's age. This wouldn't be the last time Karrie would help my mom with babysitting. When my mom got her job years later at the school, Karrie was nice enough to watch Jack everyday for free. She has always been a good friend to my mom. Scarlett and my mom were gone forever. I was starting to become really worried because what could take so long? When they finally got back I heard my mom tell Karrie that they made them sit in the waiting room so long that she left. She would take her to Dr. Fisher tomorrow, because the people at the ER apparently didn't feel like she was going to die or they would have rushed her back. Scarlett would soon have many doctor appointments and the first of three allergy tests. I wasn't there for the first one, but the one she would get at age nine turned out to become something that made her sound like she was dying. She screamed every time they scratched her back. I never want to get that test. It turned out that she was and is allergic to peanuts. Unfortunately for Scarlett, her life would always be checking labels and scratching the hives on her face and body. I have always felt really bad for her.

Between the ages of 5-8, I don't really remember a lot of things about *him*. I know there had to be the occasional hair-pulling and mean remarks. *he* always liked to pull my hair and my mom's. When I don't remember, that doesn't mean *he* didn't do it. *he* has always been mean to us all, I just don't remember anything directed towards me during those three years. *he* had taken my dog, Sam, and dropped him off at railroad tracks. My mom and us kids spent days looking for him, and we finally found him at the animal shelter. Sadly, we only had him for a short time before *he* disposed of him again.

All of us kids were very big into sports, friends, and school. Many birthdays and major events happened and *he* missed them all. I can't remember *him* ever being at birthday party for any of us. During these years, my mom was very different. When I say different, I mean she didn't stand up to *him*. She didn't speak her mind. She was always busy with volunteering at my school and transporting us all around, but she never seemed happy. I think she became *him*. Things would change soon. She would find herself and find her voice.

I think the turning point was what *he* did to Jack. I believe this happened when I was eight. Scarlett and Jack have always argued. They could never get along and probably caused my mom to have a lot of gray hairs. They had been fighting and Scarlett ran into the closet to hide from Jack. They must have been four and two at the time. Jack opened the door and I remember hearing Scarlett scream. Jack slammed the door shut and accidentally slammed Scarlett's fingers in the door. *he* just happened to be around that day and *he* grabbed Jack so hard. The thing about *him,* which you will hear me talk about many times, is that when *he* gets mad *his* eyes become huge. *he* got down into Jack's face, eyes bulging and spit coming out of his mouth, and *he* started telling Jack that he better never touch one of his kids. *he* then turned him over, pulled down his diaper and smacked him. The sound was terrible, but not as bad as Jack's cry. You could tell that *he* smacked Jack way too hard. *he* then dragged Jack by his hand upstairs and told him that he would sit in his room and think about what he had done.

My mom went running upstairs. We all went running after her. We go into Jack's room and she pulled down his pants. On his little butt was the handprint made by *him*. *He* (how I want to always refer to *him*) has the smallest hands, so they filled up Jack's whole butt cheek. My mom ran him a warm bath and *he* came in asking what she was doing. This was the day I saw a spark in her eye. This was the day that I think turned her around. This is the day she decided that she was done with the abuse.

I know that *he* had to have been mean to her when I didn't know it. It wasn't until I got a little older and *he* started doing it every day, that I really started paying attention. I started watching and listening. It would be the next part that I can write the most about. I don't remember all of what transpired during that argument. I know for a week after, Jack had a hand bruise on his butt. I know my mom must have felt bad because she swaddled him into a towel and rocked him in his bed. I know that for better or worse, this was the day that she planted her foot down and decided to no longer be a doormat. This day was a good day.

My mom is much younger than *he* is. For some reason, she had decided that she wanted to throw *him* a 40th birthday party. She spent weeks planning and I know this, because I helped. I helped her at GFS and I helped lick all the envelopes for the invitations. It was supposed to be a big party with almost 100 people invited.

Thing is, most things don't go as we plan, and this day was no different. When a person chooses to not treat others nicely, they will eventually have consequences for their actions. 15 people came that day. It was much less than that, but some of my mom's friends ended up showing up. When *he* got home and saw what happened, *he* was not happy. I mean *his* eyes were huge and *his* attitude was even bigger. *he* came inside and started throwing all the food away. I know my mom spent a lot of money on that food, because I was with her. *he* tore down decorations and popped balloons. *he* yelled at my mom and even wasn't so nice to *his* mom. The whole time that my mom's friends, Audry and Henry and the Rodgers family, were there, *he* refused to talk to them. Luke Rodgers was, of course, outside playing baseball with his kids and Jack, which is what a dad is supposed to do.

I think my mom just wanted to get the whole day over with. I know that I have always felt like I could do nothing right and I am sure she had to feel the same way. I mean, if there was a rotten peach in the fruit bowl she got screamed at for an hour. If the toaster wasn't put away, the world was ending.

It got to the cake part and by this time *his* mood had not improved. Elaina, who has always been a very messy eater, dropped icing on her white dress. As usual, my mom was telling her that it was fine, because she would get it out. But *he* didn't see it that way. *he* didn't see it as a kid mistake. *he* started calling her an idiot and a baby.

We kids started playing in the sprinkler. We played in it earlier in the day so this was our second set of clothing. Not that this part really matters, but for some reason it mattered to *him*. *he* screamed at my mom for letting us get back in the sprinkler, I mean, I guess *he* thought we should just sit around and soak in *his* awesome mood. Everyone started leaving by this time. Since there were only 15 people there, it didn't take too long for this to be accomplished.

As the last car pulled away, I turned my head to look. We were armed with squirt guns and Scarlett had taken this

The Beginning

opportunity to fire at me. Her shot was perfect and she nailed me right in my eyeball. It is another one of those moments where I feel a little guilty. It was a reaction that I couldn't stop. I screamed out, maybe more out of being shocked than pain, but it still hurt. *he* immediately snatched Scarlett up and flung her over *his* shoulder. *He* was screaming at her, at my mom, at just the air. *His* ungratefulness had reached the top. Scarlett who was scared out of her mind was screaming for my mom. My mom went running after them - this exact scene became a cycle. She ran to a scene and we chased after her. The showdown happened in the garage. She was begging with *him* to put Scarlett down or to hand her to my mom. *he* was telling how *he* would never forgive her for having a party for *him* where only 15 people came.

I still find his comment about that humorous. Had *he* just decided to be a better person, maybe more people would have dropped their plans to attend. You get what you give in life. Scarlett was the tool to punishing my mom. It was just sad that she was closest to *him*. Anyone of us could have been dangling over *his* shoulder. *he* did hand Scarlett over to my mom, but this argument was far from over. It started in the kitchen, where my mom had set Scarlett on the island to push her hair out of her face and dry her tears. *he* was almost in her face blasting insults left and right. She kissed Scarlett on the forehead and walked to the hallway. I think she was trying to lure *him* away from us. As they get to the bottom of the steps, they stop walking. I heard a weird sound and then I no longer heard my mom's voice. We all looked at each other, us kids, trying to figure out what happened.

I decided to creep down the hallway. *he* had her back up against the wall, *his* hands wrapped around her neck. Her face was changing colors and her eyes kinda looked like *his* when *he* is mad. She was grabbing at *his* shirt, at *his* face, whatever she could reach. It was then that I see her do the move she has told us to do if a guy is ever holding us. She took her knee and rams it between *his* legs. *his* hands leave

My Proclamation

her throat and *he* bent over as a groan escaped *his* mouth. My mom stood there for a few seconds. In my mind I was willing her to run. She went to slip by *him* and *he* grabbed her. She grabbed *his* shirt and it ripped. *Princess* has always been very weird about *his* clothes. If we ever pulled on *his* shirt, we would get smacked. I think that shocked *him* enough for her to escape. That was when she turned and saw me in the hallway. She saw the other three's head sticking out of the kitchen. She knew we saw, but she didn't know how much.

Some of the events that I am about to talk about might be out of order. I remember what happened, but so much happened whenever *he* was home that I can't pinpoint the exact time. All the bad memories sort of run together in my mind.

I had a friend in school named Logan. She was black. I don't say that to be mean or because I care. The color of someone's skin does not bother me and it is not something I think about when I am around people. I say this because it did bother *him*. *he* always referred to black people with the dreaded "n" word. *he* referred to women as the "b" word, people without both limbs as lefty. Elaina and I were sitting around the table talking about our friends.

Elaina secretly had a black boyfriend. My mom knew this, as did the rest of us. No one ever brought it up around *him*. Logan was getting ready to move and my heart was broken. *he* overheard our conversation and pulled a chair out to sit next to us. *he* started in talking about slavery, which I don't think *he* knows as much as *he* thinks. *he* then told us that we needed to get on board with being racists because black people do it to themselves. *he* said that they are all a bunch of criminals and they smell. Elaina and I both looked at each other - not really shocked, because we knew that *he* felt that way. I think what we were feeling was disgust. We were disgusted that a human being can be so cruel and hateful to someone else. That a person can hate someone just because of their skin color is just sick and really sad. Our neighborhood

The Beginning

had a lot of families from India. *he* didn't really select which ones *he* liked and didn't.

he hated them all. *he* hated everyone - black, female, Indian, *his* family, and *his* children. *his* little comments always made it so apparent.

I played softball for a long time. I was pretty good, but not as good as Elaina. I made the All-Star team. *he* never came to any of those games - not during my normal season nor my All-Star season. My mom made them all, though. Guess whose games *he* did attend? He came to Elaina's when she played on Sundays. We all had to get up at 6 so she could be there super early and *he* refused to ever help or come at that time because *he* had to sleep in, but *he* usually came to her games. I'm not jealous because *he* wasn't nice to her, either.

One day I was at practice, and since Elaina and I both had practice at the same time, another mom took me. We took turns each week so my mom wouldn't always miss the same kid's practice. Elaina had to have the batting helmet that had a mask on it so I had to use the one without. It was always ok and I actually liked that helmet the best because it didn't feel so confining. During one of my up at bats, I hit the ball and it came back and it hit me in the face. Basically, that was the end of my softball career. After that day I could never stay in the square and not pull my head back, because I was afraid of it happening again. My mom tried really hard to make me not be afraid. She told me stories about how she used to get hit on purpose because she was fast and if she was on the bases she would score. She bought this stick thing that had a ball on it for me to hit. She let me hit her with it to show it didn't hurt. It didn't matter though. I was never not scared. I couldn't let it go. That is how I started playing soccer.

I really wanted to be on a team, I just couldn't go further with softball. The thing about soccer is, I was really good. I wasn't a good scorer but I was really good at stealing the ball and I

My Proclamation

was good at taking it down the field and passing it to get a score. I loved my team. I loved my coaches. I had them for four seasons. My mom never missed a practice. She never missed a game. She always took me out to practice on her days off. She always cheered me on and she has many videos of her yelling and screaming. She wasn't yelling to be mean or to be "that parent" every kid hates. She was so excited for me that she would be going crazy. Until *he* came.

Before I get into this story, there is a movie that is about a red flyer wagon and an abusive father and I think it has Tom Hanks in it. It will really explain how we felt when *he* would come home. *he* didn't hit us with his belt. *he* didn't usually hit us with *his* hands. But *his* words were the things that hurt the most and *he* hit us with those all day long or whenever *he* was home.

For some reason *he* didn't feel like *he* needed to be there for our birthdays or any other things like school stuff, but *he* felt like *he* needed to come to my games. I am sure it was because my mom told *him* how good I was and I was like that piece I talked about where *he* wanted to show off and brag about me even though *he* had just called me worthless an hour before.

There is one game that stands out to me.

It was during one my 3rd grade fall season games. This game wasn't the only game where *he* constantly badgered me and put me down, but it went on for the duration of the whole game. It continued on long after the game was over.

I earlier stated that I was a good fielder. I was really good at playing defense and dribbling the ball down the field. I was NOT good at playing goalie.

The thing about goalie is, no one really wants to play it. Because of this, if no one volunteered, the coaches would make you take turns. During this game, no one's hand went into the air when the coaches asked. I knew that I was never usually asked. I think a lot of it had to do with how bad I was at it, but I also never volunteered. My teammates were my friends and I could see their concern faces when no one volunteered. I slowly raised my hand and said "Sure, I will try!"

The team we were going up against was a really good team. Besides being good, they also were really rough. They constantly liked to throw out elbows or attempt to trip you. They also had a couple of girls who could kick the ball really hard. It would be these girls who would get four goals on me before my coaches finally had enough and took me out. The first two goals they scored were because I just suck at the position. The last two goals were because I stopped trying. I stopped trying because of *him*.

The first goal should have been called a foul. It wasn't, but I had the ball in my hands when the girl came and stepped hard on my fingers. Because of the pain, I let go of the ball and she scored. The ref didn't see what happened and that made me mad. It also made *him* mad, but not at the ref, *he* was mad at me. *He* started yelling at me with *his* eyes bulging out. I heard my Mom say "It is okay Harper. You'll get the next one!" *he* yelled, "Get your head out of your ass and get the ball!" It was embarrassing.

The second goal happened because it was their best player and she could direct her shots really well. She shot to the other side of the goal, high in the net. I don't think I could have stopped it with my limited ability. I was getting really upset by this point because I knew I was going to lose the game for my team. I tried to do the nice thing and volunteer for the position, but instead I was losing it for my team.

That is what *he* never understood. I was already really upset with myself. I am harder on myself than anyone can ever be. I do not like to fail, get in trouble, and let people down. I always

My Proclamation

try my hardest at everything I do. I didn't need *him* telling me how lousy I was because I was already telling myself that. *he* started yelling louder and louder. *he* marched over to behind the goal and took a place with his arms crossed. I tried to drown out all the demeaning words *he* was yelling. I tried humming and singing to myself. Nothing seemed to work, though. *he* told me I sucked and that *he* wouldn't waste the money to let me play next season. *he* screamed that I should be sitting on the bench and I was a terrible teammate. I looked at my Mom and she looked a little ticked off, but she blew me a kiss and mouthed the words, "It will be okay". I know she didn't want to cause a scene, more than the one *he* was already causing.

he just refused to go away. *he* never said one encouraging word. Nothing positive ever entered *his* mind. *he* made it to where I then decided to not even attempt to stop the ball.

he thinks I am terrible. Fine - I will be. In that moment, I became like *him* - the exact opposite of who I ever wanted to become. But *he* has this ability to make us miserable enough that we want company. I wish now that I would have ignored *him*; that I could have had enough courage to turn around and demand *he* stop. I just couldn't overcome proving a point - just the wrong one.

The best player came running down the field. A couple of my teammates gave her some good defense, so she wasn't able to get away so easily. The elbows of her white shirt were dirty because of how aggressive she always was. I think by that point she had caused two of my friends to trip and get hurt. As I saw her running down the field, a brilliant idea popped into my head. Well, it was brilliant at the time and could have stayed that way if it had worked out perfectly. This girl kicked the ball really hard. Normally when she scores, the ball came out of the back of the net because of how hard she kicked. I still have a bruise from the last time we played from where she missed the ball and kicked my shin instead. Maybe she

The Beginning

would do me a favor and aim her kick in *his* direction. I planned to step aside and let her kick the ball as hard as possible so maybe it would shut *him* up. I hoped it would hit *him* in his big, fat, bald, head. Unfortunately, that chick didn't do me any favors. This was the one time I could have stopped it because she kicked it right between my legs.

Oh, man. That decision angered *him* more. My lack of effort caused *his* hurtful words to come spewing out of *his* mouth at a record pace. I don't even think *he* took time to breathe it was such a mouth full. "You suck Harper! You suck at life! You have no athletic ability at all!" My coaches let me get one more score on me and then they finally took me out as goalie.

I managed to assist in two goals after that, but my team still lost. My team lost because of me and because of *him*. I hate to blame people for my mistakes or because of things I am not good at because, really, those things are my fault. In this case, *he* was able to cause me to play my worst. *he* was able to get into my head and make me not want to win, to help my team, and to just be myself. I wished I could have been a better goalie. It is scary standing in that box having people kick a fast ball at you with everyone else yelling and running in your direction. I tried to listen to my mom and the voice inside my head telling myself that I tried to do a nice gesture for my teammates. I tried to save them from having to play goalie. That voice lasted until we got home.

As soon as the engine shut off in the garage, *he* jumped out of the car and grabbed a ball. *he* told me to get my ass across to the school, which is right across the street from our house. *he* told me we would practice until I learned how to play soccer. That day was a day long before my mom stepped in and told *him* to stop. She still talked to *him* in "private" at that time, begging *him* to stop treating us like dogs. Those conversation always ended with *him* yelling in her face, "I am an asshole, that is who I was born to be! You will not tell me how to parent, you welfare bitch!" He said other things to her, too, but that was the most popular one.

My Proclamation

My mom grabbed everyone else and proposed we have a family soccer game to make it fun. I know she was trying to lighten the mood. She offered to play goalie, which I said a thank you to God for. It wasn't fun at all, though. It was *him* talking about *himself* and how good *he* was at everything (*his* favorite past time) and how I suck at everything. It was about me being a loser, worthless. A lot of it was when my mom couldn't hear.

I remember it being windy that day and the field was long. It was also normally when *he* was taking the ball from me, so *he* would get in my face with his bulging, crazy eyes and his creepy voice - the voice that gives me nightmares to even hear. Scarlett had to use the restroom, so my mom walked her home. My other two siblings followed after her, something that is really common of us. It was when she crossed the street that *he* really let me have it. I swear, spit was flying out at lightning speed. A nerve was coming out of *his* forehead and neck. It was then I refused to play anymore. It was then I knew I would never let *him* attend another game with me playing. It was then I knew that I would hate *him* forever. It was then when I started really paying attention.

I have been in a talent show at my school twice. We had a big plan for 5th grade, but because of everything else that was going on around us, we just couldn't pull it off. The first time, *he* came. The second time I made my mom promise to not tell *him*. I refused to participate if *he* attended. My mom used to be a big Kelly Clarkson fan. On one of the finales of American Idol, Kelly Clarkson did this really cool interpretation of 'People like Us'. There were glow sticks and her outfit was glow-in-the-dark. My mom has always been very good at making outfits, putting on parties, and pulling off things such as this. She brought two of our friends in and we went right to work. My mom made all of our costumes. They all were glow-in-the-dark. She purchased black lights and glow sticks for all of the audience. She bought glow-in-the-dark balls for them to throw around. It was supposed to be awesome. She talked to the mom putting it on and we got to go last. Everything was lined up to go off fantastically, except *he* decided to attend.

The Keifer's were the kids that were in the show with us. My mom was really good friends with their mom, Lucy, so she came over beforehand to have a drink and chill with my mom. *he* did not like my mom hanging out with friends. *he* was not happy that she came over to our house. *he* didn't come out and say it to Lucy, but instead *he* took it out on us. It got so bad that Elaina peed her pants before we left. She had to grab her shoes and she just peed everywhere. *he* always made Elaina have those reactions. Sometimes it was rapid blinking. Other times she would do this weird head tilt. This time it just happened that she had to pee. That angered *him* more and it just set us up to fail in his mind before we even got there. The show went off without a hitch. We rocked out the house. I have gotten compliments on that show for years now. Why is it that *he* couldn't see how great we were? After all, we are not Kelly Clarkson and we do not have millions of dollars to put on a production like she does. When we got home *he* just started tearing it apart. We didn't sing loud enough. We didn't jump enough. We didn't sound good enough. The bottom line was, we were just never good enough.

Around the age of 6, I decided I wanted to be a doctor. This is probably a pretty normal profession for little kids to choose. I wanted to be an ER doctor because I thought it seemed exciting and fast-paced and interesting. My love for reading began around this time too, so I added writer to this list. My mom would always say, "Become a doctor first, then a writer!" My love for medical care only lasted a short time when I stumbled upon my real passion. It has always had to do with helping others. This would just be in a different manner. My mom started putting Shark Tank on at night when we were getting ready for bed. I was very interested in the inventions and the sharks themselves. My sisters, brother, and I started play court at home. There were always certain jobs we always

My Proclamation

seemed to fall into. Attorney would be mine. Becoming an attorney would become my new dream. For a long time I felt like being a patent attorney was the path I should take. I wanted to major in engineering and then attend law school. I read that they make a really good living and I just really enjoyed working with electronics and learning about new creations.

My mom has always been very supportive of us all. If we wanted to try a new sport, she's say, "Sure, let's do it." If Jack asked for an ATM machine for Christmas (which he did), she helped him write a letter to Santa - my other parent, not so much. As soon as *he* got whiff of the fact that I wanted to be a lawyer, it was game on. *he* has told me that I would grow up to be a liar, that I would grow up and live under a bridge (this might very much happen a few years later). I would grow up and be worthless. These insults and jabs never stopped. I didn't really understand how a patent attorney could really lie anyway, but *he* never seemed to care, and of course, always had to be downright mean and made to feel like *he* was right. It wouldn't be until a few years later when someone stumbled into my life to change my dream.

I have always believed in right and wrong. I have always believed that laws are there to help a country work (even though I question some of them now). I just didn't know until she walked into my life that what I really needed to do was practice a completely different type of law. I didn't know that what I really wanted to do was stand up for children like us and stop the corrupt fathers who treat us all like crap. It would be just a few years later when I would start demanding truth and seeking justice. It would be a couple years later when my whole life would be turned upside down and I learned that the Justice System that was designed to protect us was completely flawed.

My elementary school has been the best school for us all to attend. We have had some issues with girls being extremely mean and some parents being completely negligent. For example, sending a jar of peanut butter with their kid for snack time, when their child is in a peanut-free room. Shame on you people for not taking that allergy seriously. My sister could die if she consumed peanuts, and sadly, the only way for you people to care or understand that is if it happens to you. My mom made fast friends with a couple of our teachers at the school. It became her home away from home. I know because of conversations that I overheard about how my mom sometimes had a say in our teachers, and two, certain teachers she wanted us all to have. Besides a few times, the second never happen. Mrs. Nash became a really good friend of my mom's. Elaina, my older sister, had her for second and third grade. My mom still to this day feels like Mrs. Nash is one of the best people she knows and one of the best teachers. My mom's plan was for me to have Mrs. Nash also. During my second grade year, Mrs. Nash had already moved to 3rd grade. Mrs. Spencer was chosen for me for that year. I didn't know at the time how instrumental this would be in my life.

Certain people come into our lives and make such an impact, and she would become one of those people. I had already started becoming thirsty for knowledge before I entered her classroom. She just further set me on that path. She helped me see my potential. She made me truly believe in myself. She once told me that I was born the change the world and she had a way of making me believe this. By the end of the school year, it had been decided that Mrs. Spencer was going to move up to third grade and I would have the opportunity to have her again. We got a letter sent home with us to rather agree or opt out of it. See, my mom loves Mrs. Spencer. As time as gone by and she has had the time to really get to know her, my mom absolutely loves her. Yet, remember the plan was for me to always have Mrs. Nash. For two weeks my mom and I talked about that letter. I was dead set that I was going to have her again for a second year. I told my mom that there would be no way that I would turn that letter into her with

My Proclamation

it not signed. I think that my mom really looked to see what was in the best interest of me.

I would later hear her tell *him,* while *he* was screaming at her for this decision, that she made the right decision for me not for her. That Elaina had a relationship with Mrs. Nash like I had with Mrs. Spencer and she was the right choice for me. We had this conversation at a Buffalo Wild Wings on the way to another dreadful beach vacation. *he* was extremely mad at my mom for not doing as *he* suggested. This was nothing new, though, and I was super glad she didn't follow *his* demands. During that whole dinner *he* got Elaina so riled up. See, Elaina loved Mrs. Nash like I loved Mrs. Spencer. Elaina idolized her just the same as me. *he* told Elaina so many lies during that dinner and *he* made her still, to this day, believe things that aren't true. So what happened next is solely *his* fault even though Elaina is responsible for herself.

When we got up to leave, she came over and punched me in the throat. She told me I made a big mistake. During the process of my brain telling my body to gasp for air, I remember thinking, "No, you did. You decided to become like *him*!"

The trip to Buffalo Wild Wing was not by accident. We were on our way to Myrtle Beach. This summer vacation trip became something that happened every two years and caused many different emotions inside me. It was a week-long trip that had a few fun times, but was mostly made of up of days of misery. *he* was never equipped to be a dad. *he* didn't like to spend 20 minutes with us let alone 7 days.

Our family once tried to take a vacation to the Outer Banks. I think that trip had the potential to be a great trip. It just was never given the chance. We went with *his* family. Well, just *his* mommy and daddy (his name for them, not mine). We would be in the pool swimming and *he* would just stand there and stare with his arms crossed, a scowl on his face. *he* would

The Beginning

complain that the water was too cold, the sand was to rocky, the ocean was too far away, even though we had a house on the beach. *he* complained of the food, the grocery store, the drive, and us bastards. *he* scolded my mom, *he* called her worthless and a fat "b" word. I remember the whole trip we had planned to go see the wild horses. It is on my mom's bucket list and it is something that we kids really wanted to do. It was really the reason why we decided to go there.

The last minute, *he* got grumpy and *he* refused to let us do it. *he* refused to give my mom the money to do so. Even though this was a bit disappointing because it was supposed to be the highlight of our trip, it was another event that sticks out in mind. We were all pretty upset that *he* had decided to punish us that day. *he* then decided that we were going to go over to this island and walk around and fish (blah, blah, because that is what *he* wanted to do). We drove forever to get on the hour boat ride to take us across. I don't know what *he* expected from us, but we were little kids and weren't too excited about the trip. *he* was being very short and jerking us around as we walked.

At one time I looked over and I could see my mom saying something to *him* about it. I couldn't hear it because of the wind and motor of the boat, but I could tell by her hand gestures. So the best part of this is, *he* had decided that because of our attitudes, we were going to not attend the island. We were going to ride the boat back for another hour and go back to our house. Sounds super fun, right? By the time we got back to our car, we were all in terrible moods. It was the tone of the trip. *he* got behind the wheel and gassed the car really fast. Elaina gets motion sickness and I remember her making a little squeal because of it. I don't know how fast *he* was going and at the time I don't think I thought of that question. I just remember how fast everything outside was going by. I then notice something from the window. We were on the other side of the road. I look up out the front window of the car and up ahead was a car and *he* was driving right at it really fast. I heard my mom scream and she yelled "Please, Stop!" I was so scared at the moment and the look on my mom's face let me know that she was too. I really think she thought that was it for us all, just like I did. I don't know what happened, but *he* swerved back over, while our lives were flashing before our eyes.

This trip to Myrtle Beach was something that *he* demanded we do. It would be the first vacation we would take by ourselves. No one from his family would be attending or anyone from my Mom's. I don't think the events of this vacation would have been prevented even if someone else was there. Where *he* usually tried to hide who *he* was when others were around, it always seemed hard for *him* to do after so many days. *he* had started a few months before calling Elaina a traitor anytime she would spend time with my Mom. If *he* walked into the room and she didn't like bow to *him*, she would get called a traitor.

That is the thing about *him, he* always expected some special treatment. *he* always told us we owed *him*. Not that we asked to be brought in this world and it wasn't like my Mom didn't teach us to be grateful. We have always had manners and used them all the time. It was like *he* felt like we should idolize *him* but *he* never gave us any reason to have those feelings. *he* always demanded respect and always, ALWAYS told us that we were not respectful (this would cause me triggers years down the road). Toward the end of *his* time in our house, my mom would always tell *him* that respect is earned, not demanded.

During this whole trip, if Elaina decided to hang out with my Mom, *he* would call her that. *he* would refuse to come out of the hotel saying that *he* didn't want to be in the sun. I remember my mom saying "you mean the sun... at the beach?" So my mom, who actually likes to live a fun life, would take us out to the beach. She turned us all into mermaids by making us tails out of sand. We would take long

The Beginning

walks to hunt for treasures, sharks teeth or seashells. There was this go kart racing place there that we always visited. The thing that was always kinda weird about *him* was that *he* would kinda be in an okay mood, but as soon as we got in the car, *he* would instantly change. This happened to be the case that day.

It was a little drive to the place. I remember feeling excitement as we got out of the car. We have so many pictures at this place so our minds were soaked with memories. When we walked into the place, we walked up the counter to pay. It was almost a playback of the wild horses incident last trip. *he* instantly demanded that we leave. *he* said that *he* would not pay for us to do that and we need to all get into the car right that second. My mom, who was fed up with *his* negative attitude and another vacation flushed down the toilet, refused to leave. She said that we were all excited to participate and drive cars and we were not going to leave.

See, my dad liked to take my mom's bank card. *he* liked to control people whenever *he* could. It wasn't like she would just hand it over when *he* would demand it. *he* would find it when she was sleeping or busy with us. She would later learn to sleep with it under her pillow (which she doesn't know I know this) or she would lock it in her car and hide her keys. On this day she had her card. On this day she put her foot down. It might sound dumb. It might sound like she refused to back down. The thing about my story is, I am picking a handful of events that led to where we are now.

You have to remember, every day where *he* was involved, was torture. My mom gave in too much. My mom was tortured too much. My mom got to a breaking point, too. *he* said "Fine, see you f'ers" and *he* left. *he* took the car and left. I remember my mom looking out the window watching *him* go. We were all wrapped around her, not sure how we were going to get home. I looked up at her and asked what was going to happen. She said "we are going to ride go karts right now,

My Proclamation

Harper. Maybe our next adventure will be riding a taxi to the airport and flying on a plane. Either way, we are going to have a good day," and we did!! *he* returned some time later. My mom made amends with *him*. She bought *him* a wrist band and watched the little two so we could all ride. The thing to know about *him* is, if *he* isn't having fun, no one is!

It was during this trip that I got stung by a jellyfish. I can't really explain the pain but I remember a burning feeling on my leg. I remember being in the ocean having fun and all of a sudden, this extremely painful feeling coming over my leg. I love the ocean and the beach, but that will be the last time I ever go into water I cannot see in. I had several welts on the back of my leg. These welts were similar to the ones *he* came home from an hour trip to the grocery store with. The thing about my welts were, they looked like tentacles. I had three or four on the back of my calf. *his* were on *his* back and they were in the shape of a hand print. *he* also had scratches on the other side. I always found this to be such a mystery.

They had this big pirate show in Myrtle Beach. They served you this unbelievable dinner and the show was amazing. When we arrived at the theater, Elaina and I seated ourselves on both sides of my mom. That left Scarlett and Jack to be with *him*. It didn't last the whole time. We would all eventually work our way next to my mom. It was the only way to enjoy anything. *he* had asked Elaina if she wanted to trade with Jack. When she replied with a no, *he* called her a traitor again. The show was amazing. It had so many stunts, cannons, and a sea lion. It lasted long into the evening and way past our bedtime. By the time it was over, Scarlett and Jack were really tired. When neither one of them were in school my mom would still make them take naps. The drive back to our condo was really far. We stayed at the top of Myrtle Beach. Almost at the very tip so anytime we went anywhere it involved a long car ride. By the time we arrived into the garage, both of them were sleeping.

The Beginning

We unloaded the car and my mom had asked my, well *him*, which one *he* wanted to carry. *he* said "wake their asses up, they can walk," *he* was not going to carry either one of them. My mom grabbed them both. I don't remember what floor we stayed on but it was pretty high because we had a really good view of the ocean and we were not allowed to go on the balcony without my mom. She made it almost to the door with them both. She was in really good shape then. By this time Jack had woken up. I think my mom literally couldn't carry them both anymore. Since Jack was awake she set him down right by the door as we were walking in. She told us that she was going to lay Scarlett down and then she would put Jack in bed. Jack was like three at the time. He wanted my mom and he was tired. He laid down on the floor right in front of the door and started crying. *he* started screaming at Jack. At any time *he* could have picked Jack up and carried him to bed. I was like 7 and I knew the way to problem solve this matter. Instead, *he* started calling him "Sally". *he* told "Sally" to move his ass and get out of the doorway. Right as my mom walked out of the room, *he* took his foot and kicked Jack in the head. Jack went flying out of the doorway down the hall. The sound this made was not good. I am sure some of it had to do with my heart beating in my chest and the fear inside my body. I know he made a sound and my mom did too. She came running. We would never take another trip with *him*.

When we returned home from our trip, most things returned to normal. *he* wasn't home a lot and when *he* was, it was bad like always. Welfare, worthless, losers, living under a bridge. Pay when we get older, idiots, losers. The insults never stopped. The threats were always provided. When we returned, that was when I started distancing myself further from *him*. I witnessed *him* strangle my mom, kick my brother in the head, almost kill us with our car and so on and so on. *he* was making our house miserable. *he* was making us all hate ourselves and *he* was trying to make us hate others.

My Proclamation

One day Jack was running around the house. He had shot his little sticky frog up onto the ceiling and my mom, who does forget things, didn't get it down immediately. It left a stain on the ceiling. This led to a 30 minute speech about how we don't appreciate anything and how we can't have anything nice. *he* tried to grab Jack to spank him. Jack started running from *him*. We had an island in our kitchen and our table. It was really funny because *he* couldn't catch Jack. I think Jack felt like he was running for his life. *he* always used baby powder. I am not sure where or why or how but *he* would always have it on *his* pants. *he* went and grabbed it and sat down at the table.

We eventually forgot about *him* and went back to playing. Jack walked by *him* to get his drink on the counter and *he* took a handful of baby powder and threw it in Jack's face. My mom was in shock. Jack gasped for air. My mom ran to Jack and said "Are you serious?" to which *he* replied "You said I can't hit him anymore," with a smirk on *his* face. It was that summer also when Jack, who has a perfectly good name, was officially no longer called by it. *he* started calling Jack "Sally" and "faggot" on daily basis. "Come tell me goodbye "Sally", quit crying like a little "faggot", come over here so I can beat your ass "Sally"." We have a lot of friends that have all boys. Our friend, Donovan, who we always wished was our dad was always playing with his two boys. I always thought it was so weird that it was my mom who taught Jack how hit a baseball, how to throw a football, and how to ride a bike.

Jack has always had a really big heart. He and I are very much alike. We like to help people and we do cry at movies. Jack cries at every movie. *he* hated it. Jack feels compassion for the guy whose arm was gone. *he* hated it, *he* called him lefty. *he* has never liked Jack and *he* has never hidden it.

The school year went fast. I was in third grade, Elaina in 5th grade, and Scarlett in 1st. Elaina was being tutored by Mrs. Nash for reading. *he* hated it. Elaina started telling Mrs. Nash about what was going on in our house. *he* told Elaina that *he* thought it was terrible that my mom was making her be tutored. *he* told her that it was a waste of time. She needed to focus on math and science.

We found pictures of naked girls on our computer. We only saw them for a second, but it also happened on YouTube. *he* was getting ready to go to work one weekend when we were all around the island with my mom. We were watching YouTube videos of Jojo Siwa when all of a sudden *he* said, "She is so fat and ugly and guys should feel sorry for her!" *he* then said that we were wasting our time watching her fat ass. My mom told *him* that she is like a millionaire. and a child. She doesn't need our pity and Mom said that they have both gained weight from when they were younger and they shouldn't be putting kids down. *his* response would be educational. *he* said, "Oh yeah, I'm the government and you are welfare!" My mom asked what that was supposed to mean. *he* said, "You are all a bunch of leeches and if it wasn't for me, you would all be dead!" *he* then brought up us being homeless and living under a bridge. *he* stormed out of the house and slammed the door behind *him*.

One day we were playing outside with our neighbors when *his* daddy showed up. My mom sat down for a long time talking with him. She had tears going down her face. She sent us outside, but when I came in to go the bathroom, I could see her makeup down her face. She asked me to tell him about all the things *he* had said about me wanting to be a lawyer, about all the names *he* had called me. We were going to go to Zoombezi that day and *he* was supposed to meet us there. My grandpa left with *his* guns. *he* talked through the camera asking where he was going. We ended up going to Zoombezi. *he* wanted us to wait on *him* but *he* was mad about the guns and *he* said *he* couldn't be there until almost closing time, so my mom decided that *he* could meet us there. It didn't end up that way. *he* was mad that my grandpa took the guns. *he* was mad that we didn't wait for *him*. We had a good time while we

My Proclamation

were there, but we didn't go home. *he* called my mom 50 times and I could hear *him* screaming. I could hear *him* calling her names that I didn't even know the meaning of. I could hear *him* threatening her life and threatening to take us away.

During the drive to my grandparents' house, where we stayed for many days, I was playing on my mom's phone. We had a security camera on our doorbell. You could ring the doorbell and your face would pop up on my mom's phone and inside the house. You could talk to the person and the person could talk to you. It was that night that I saw some gross stuff. It was that night that *he* pulled *his* pants down and showed *his* boy parts. It was that night that I saw too much and it was that night I puked in my mouth. We stayed in Mom's Hometown for like a week and then we went home and things went back to the way the used to be. Living in a home where we felt trapped.

My mom spent that whole year at the school every day doing the bookroom. Jack would come too and she would have lunch with us all many times each week. She was babysitting, too. His name was Landon and she would sometimes bring him with her.
My mom watched his sister and his cousin. His cousin's name was Josie. My mom would grow to love her like us. She and my mom became really close. Josie would go everywhere with us. She went to the library and to the zoo. Her grandma was Mrs. Clemens and she worked at our school. My mom became really good friends with her and we would go to her house a lot. Josie lived with her grandma because her dad and mom were having some struggles and it wasn't good for Josie to live with them then. Josie is really lucky to have Julia. I don't think she likes our family anymore but my mom always really cared for their whole family. We all did.

Christmas Eve was always a big deal in our house. We would have our house packed with people and Santa from the zoo would come and bring presents to everyone. It was a big party

27

and usually a good time. This Christmas Eve was different. No one talked to my mom. Now when I think back to it, no one really talked to my mom since my grandpa was in our house that day. My mom was always really close to a couple of *his* sisters. *his* brother, Brad, would come up and bring his kids and hang out with my mom. I have never really been fond of any of them. They all just bash everyone. They bash each other. Their best pastime is sitting and talking bad about everyone. They use the "n" word to talk about blacks. The call gays what *he* likes to call Jack. They hate poor people or people that are on welfare. They talk about politics too much.

They think they are really important and instead, they are really hateful people. *his* mommy has called me a brat. She has called me several bad names. *his* daddy burnt my cousin in the eye with his cigar. *he* used to let us play in the cupboard with the chemicals when my parents weren't there. They talk bad about their own kids. The rest of his family doesn't watch their kids. My mom was always with us and she became like a babysitter or something. One day when we were there for pizza night, it was a hot summer night. *he* wasn't there because you know, but the rest of *his* family was. My mom was still being treated fake at this time. I am sure as soon as she left, they would bash her, too. They had a pool out for us kids to play in. My cousin, who was little, fell into the pool face down. She was really little maybe 1 or 2 at the time. If it wasn't for my mom watching, and Elaina and me knowing about how easy it is to drown, things could have gone really bad. Sadly, *his* family never learned their lesson. I am just glad that I am no longer a guinea pig for their experiments.

Santa always brought us one big present. This year, even though the whole night was off, the biggest present under the tree had all four of our names on it. My mom was super excited for us to open this present. Even though no one had spoken to her this whole night, she managed to get all of their attention to watch us open this box. The big box ended up having multiple boxes in it. Now that I know how Christmas

My Proclamation

works, I know that this was my mom's doing. She was always a really good gift-giver. She always put a lot of thought into things. I know this not only because I have watched her do it, but also because she has taught us to do it. The first box had CDs in it. They were of Paula Abdul, Boyz 2 Men and New Kids on the Block. We all had been watching Fuller House and News Kids on the Block were on it. We all were digging NKOTB then. The next Box had New Kids t-shirts in it. We all put them on.

The next box had mine and Elaina's names on it with a note for us to read. I don't remember what the notes said, but when we opened the box it had 6 tickets inside for us to go see them in concert. The four of us screamed. We jump up and down. Besides my type-writer and my lawyer bag, this was probably the best gift I have ever gotten. Our excitement was short-lived. I guess *he* was not very happy about the gift. *he* dropped a glass in the kitchen, and *he* made some nasty remarks about it. Even though there was a ticket for *him*, *he* made it clear that *he* was not going. *he* made it clear to my mom that *he* didn't think we should go. And then *he* drank another beer.

There had been some nights before Christmas Eve when I would wake up and there would be something pushed in front of the door. My mom would tell us that something dropped behind the dresser and she had to get it. I haven't asked her about those comments, but I think it was her way to not let on to what was going on. Around the time of *his* 40th birthday party, where *he* strangled my mom, we all started sleeping in the same room. *he* worked at night. Scarlett and Jack usually ended up with my mom anyway. I slowly started having nightmares and anxiety about my mom and about how crazy *he* was. It was Elaina who followed us last. She didn't really figure out who *he* was until the end.

That night before we went upstairs *he* started yelling at my mom. My mom's brother, Graham, was at the party and he and my mom were talking about some guys they both knew and how they both knew them. On our way to bed *he* started calling her a whore and accusing her of cheating. I think my mom was drained because of how the night went. My parents used to own a house in Lancaster and they just sold it. The only thing any of them said to my mom was when his dad said to her "Are you the honey with the money? Barry told me to tell you to write me a check for like $7000." I remember my mom just ignoring *his* remarks about her being a whore. I didn't even know what that meant at the time.

That night, something got put in front of the door. I am unsure if anyone heard *him*. We always sleep with a tv on. It became even more important after this date. It would help drown out the beatings on the door. It would help drown out *his* threats and *his* demands. That night, it didn't drown it out for me. I am unsure if my mom was just really tired and slept through it, or maybe she just chose to not care that night. I just couldn't drown it out and it might be the fact that it went on for hours. It was this day that makes me think that my fear of doors and locks and windows began. I bet this wasn't the first day that *he* did this, but it is the first day that I remember. This is the night that sticks out in my mind as being the first night of the last night that I really ever slept. It would also be the last night that I would ever see my mom sleep again.

Where the school year went really fast and is mostly a blur, is the time frame that I remember the most. I remember the constant beating on the door. The threats about *him* killing her. The threats about how we would never see her again. *he* would still tell us we would be homeless. *he* was still taking her car keys and card when she got careless for one second. My mom was losing a lot of weight. She was puking all the time. Elaina had to take a break from tutoring. *he* claimed that because of Elaina telling Mrs. Nash about what was going on in our home, that my mom said that the principal was going to do something about it. I really wished that were true. It was a really weird time because it was like I wanted no one to know but I also wanted everyone to know. The bigger the secret, the less likely we would ever get help.

The summer that I was going into fourth grade was the summer *he* started hanging around the house more. It was absolutely terrible. Most nights, the only time we would see *him* would be when we got home late from a sport. We would walk in to eat a quick dinner or go to bed and *he* would be sitting there in the dark, *his* arms crossed, eyes bulging, a frown on *his* face. *he* would usually not speak unless *he* felt like we had done something fun that day. Those days would result in what I would consider a twenty question day. We would be asked "where were you, who were you with, what did you do, what did you eat, who did you see, etc." *he* didn't ask these questions because *he* cared. I can't prove that, of course, but it was done in a way like *he* was trying to find something out. It was done with a tone to *his* voice that was unfriendly. It was never done with a sound of *him* really caring. It got to be where we didn't want to tell *him* anymore. It got to be to the point where I really just wanted *him* to leave. Instead, our house became the local hangout. The day that *he* started being home more was around the same time that there was always someone at our house.

One summer evening my mom had 4 or 5 friends over. All of their kids were there, too. They would drink wine or have drink and we would order pizza or cookout and play kickball or water games. This was the day *he* was home. I remember Melinda Newsom was there. She used to be my mom's good friend. Her husband, David, had just died from cancer and she doesn't really talk to any of us anymore. It is crazy to me because my mom spent so much time with both of them for a long time. She was hanging out with my mom and her other friends when *he* came up and *he* asked about their vacation. *he* said that we wouldn't get to go on vacation because *he* is just an asshole. Melinda didn't say anything after that. We were all hanging out around the table eating when Elaina opened the door and told mom to come upstairs in a hurry. My mom got up and ran upstairs fast and I followed after her.

One of the kids had turned on the water in the bathroom sink and left it on, so it was going all over the floor. My mom shut it off and grabbed a bunch of towels. As she was starting to clean up the mess, *he* came around the corner. My mom had this really cool blow dryer that had like leopard print on it or something and it was green. She got it as a gift from one of her friends that worked at Penzone's Hair Salon. *he* grabbed it and threw it on the wet towels. At this time all the kids were up there watching. She grabbed it and said something like, "This shouldn't be on wet towels". *he* said, "I know more about electrical shit than you ever will, you stupid cunt." (I'm sorry I am using bad words, but you have to hear it) *he* then started in about it not being her house and how it is only *his* house and how she can get out blah, blah, blah. *he* started calling her names. All of the kids and myself were hearing it. I remember feeling embarrassed and ashamed. Why didn't *he* understand that it was embarrassing for our friends to hear his hatred towards us. My mom just walked downstairs. *he* asked her if she was going to finish cleaning it up and she just said that it isn't her house and *he* could go ahead. We all went back outside, and I think she tried to let it go.

I forgot about it for the rest of the night. I forget about it most days. I didn't know what that word meant, the word that *he* called her. I still don't really understand it. I have looked it up even though my mom told me to not worry about it. She told me that it is just a nasty word and that it should never be said. It is just another word added to the list of words *he* has taught us.

Sometime close to my mom's birthday, I noticed she had a big bruise on her knee. When I asked her what happened, because it was so big and it looked terrible, she had just mentioned that it happened during soccer. My mom would always play goalie during our soccer games with all our

My Proclamation

friends. Somehow she is really fast and she is not afraid of the ball. I thought it was weird that she got a bruise from that though, because I knew where she was hit with the ball and it was not near her knee. It was much higher on her leg and she was only hit in the leg once and not by a hard kick. I didn't question her answer. I very rarely questioned what I was told, until the rest of the story unfolded.

A few weeks later would be a night that would forever haunt me. I remember asking a friend recently, if they knew what fear feels like. Not like the fear of having someone jump out and yell "boo", but actual fear. How your own heart pounding in your chest sounds and how the air around you changed. This night *he* had been beating on the door for hours. I think *he* probably kicked it a couple times, also. I really didn't understand what his point was in all of that. If *he* wanted in, why not just kick the door down? I think that *he* really just wanted to scare us. It was *his* way to control us and to keep us filled with fear.

Lucy, our dog, had been pacing by the door for hours. She was doing that because it was her way of telling my mom that she needed to go to the bathroom. My mom must have been waiting for *him* to cool down before she unlocked the door and went out. By the time that happened, everyone was fast asleep. I am sure my mom thought I was asleep too. I remember feeling her move and get out of bed. She grabbed her phone from under her pillow. I heard the door open and then shut seconds later. I don't know why I felt like following her. Part of me wishes that that memory was not forever part of my brain. I watched *him* drag my mom down the hallway towards *his* bedroom, while at the same time punching her over and over. Watching my mom twist and turn and also trying to punch *him* to get free. The sounds that came from her mouth are sounds that always come into my dreams. The sound of the dog barking, the look on *his* face, the coldness that I felt surround me and the concrete that surrounded my feet. I don't know why and I hate myself for it, but I couldn't make myself move. The yell that was in the back of my throat could not escape. The fists that I wanted to use would not form. I just stood there frozen in time, unable to do anything to help her. If I could change anything in my life, it would be that one moment.

I have learned how to fight back. I have learned how to use my voice. I just wish that my voice would have been used that night, that I could have stopped her nightmares and saved her body from *his* blows. I have learned through this process that wishing doesn't get you anywhere and you cannot change the past. I struggle with those two things a lot.

The next morning when I got up, I grabbed her phone and turned on the flashlight. I got under the blanket and I looked at her legs. A sickness filled my stomach. What I witnessed on her legs was a sight that I had only seen in movies and not many movies at that. At that time, I was not allowed to watch anything worse than PG13. I laid there with so much guilt inside me. My eyes watered up. I prayed to God for forgiveness and in my mind I begged for hers. The thing about that is that she didn't know that I was standing in the shadows. I wonder if she would have fought harder had she seen me. Would *he* have stopped if *he* had seen me? *he* has never liked me. Maybe *he* would have beaten me, too. I laid there until she woke up. I pretended to be asleep and watched her struggle to get out of bed. She managed to put a smile on her face and made it through the day. There were many times during the day when I would glance at her and I would notice tears in her eyes. I tried to be extra helpful that day. Everyone asked her what happened and she said that she went to let the dog out and she slipped and fell down the steps. She does have a habit of doing that so I think she thought we would believe her. I wished with everything I had that I could. Even though I wanted to call her out right then, I kept her secret. I kept it for months. I wasn't sure when the time would come for me to let it out of the bag and the way it happened wasn't how I would have planned it.

My Proclamation

Soccer and Field Hockey season were approaching. School was getting ready to start. My mom had taken us to Easton on her birthday to go school shopping. It is sad that my mom never really celebrated her birthday. She celebrates us instead. We got to eat at one of our favorite restaurants, Adobe Gila. *he* hadn't been able to get her keys or her card for a while. It was about a week later when *he* decided to make a bigger decision. I think *he* had decided that she had outsmarted him with hiding her keys and card. *he* wasn't punishing us any longer. She went to take us to the orthodontist. We had retainers and the dog had eaten mine. She went to pay for my new retainer and her card was declined. I could see the look of panic and embarrassment on her face. I think she also had to know that *he* was up to something. I was a little worried because I didn't want my teeth to shift. I had braces for a year and I was hoping to keep them straight.

My mom just did what she always does, she would just shrug it off and said she would figure it out. It wasn't for a couple of weeks that I was able to put the whole thing together. The food at home became less and less available. I had to miss soccer practice because I had no cleats to wear. There were a couple of days when our stomachs growled so bad that we shed some tears. We started having dinner with friends. If *he* got her keys, we would walk. The unbelievable thing about all of this is that *he* would bring home a pizza and some beer and sit there and eat it in front of us. The smell would cause our stomachs to growl even louder. Never once would *he* offer any one of us a slice, all the while our mouths were watering. *he* would ask us to go out to dinner and when we would plead with my mom to not make us go with *him*, *he* would just punish us more. Going out to dinner was a couple hours of elbows being pushed into our sides and our nerves being so high because we could not drop or spill anything. *his* name calling would become so loud that it would make me want to

The Beginning

sink far down into my seat. It got to where my mom had reached her end.

My grandma was up to stay the night. I think it was because my mom was not sleeping, she was not eating, and she was puking a lot. I remember *him* walking into our room and asking for some records of an account. She gave them to *him* and they had a little disagreement. She begged and pleaded for *him* to give it back. *he* told her to never do it again and she told *him* to stop threatening her. She begged for *him* to buy us food and told *him* we needed items for school. *he* just blamed her. *he* said that she was making *him* punish us all. It was her fault we were hungry. It was her fault that we couldn't play our sports. It was her fault for being such a worthless bitch. *he* called her welfare and *he* told her she deserved it. *he* said we all did. That would be the last time I can remember seeing them talk and I thank God every day for that.

The Middle

My fourth-grade year had started. Elaina had orientation and was at the middle school now. It felt weird to not have her in my school anymore. Jack started kindergarten and so my mom would be home by herself some days. It was the first year she never had one of us home. She cried a lot that first day of school, not in front of Jack, but when I stepped into the bathroom to brush my teeth I found her sitting there with tears streaming down her face. She always had one of us by her side and now she would be alone with *him*. I bet some of those tears were because of that. One weekend a few weeks into school we all decided to have a family meeting. When I say we, I mean the five of us. We had a meeting in our bedroom closet. Our closet was the size of a small bedroom. It could fit two small mattresses and many toys and clothes. We all went into the closet, alone with our mom. My mom asked how we were all doing. She asked why we were having the meeting and how we were feeling. We kids had already decided how the meeting was going to play out. We knew what we had to do. We had to tell her, we had to let her know it was time. We told her to make *him* leave. We told her that we were scared and that we knew. We told her that it had to be done. We let her know that we couldn't continue living like that another day.

The next couple weeks are a blur. We were almost like on the run. We spent a lot of time with different people at different houses. The weekend after we told her, we dog sat for Julia Clemens. Her family went to her sister's wedding in Michigan so we took care of her house and her pets. *he* called my mom the whole night. *he* sent Elaina texts to my mom's phone. *he*

The Middle

made threats. Mrs. Nash took us to lunch. She took us shopping for clothes. She made us forget for a few hours. We went to Karrien's, The Thompson's, my grandparents' house, and my mom's "friend", Alexis. We even went to Mrs. Simon's house. We had to miss school and stay away from our house. It was the night at Mrs. Simon's house that something happened. My mom doesn't tell me many things so I have to figure them out for myself. We were planning on sleeping there overnight when all of a sudden something happened and we were finally allowed to go home. I remember walking into my house that night being a little scared. The house was a mess. There were beer cans everywhere and empty fast food containers. There was still no food in the refrigerator.

My mom is really weird about smells. She likes things to smell good and so our house always did. That night when we walked in, it smelled. It smelled of old food, the dog, and of *him*. The first night I don't think any of us slept. We were finally allowed to go back to school. My mom had a conversation with us about *him*. She told us that *he* went to stay somewhere else and that for now *he* had to stay away. She said that if we saw *him* we had to tell an adult and that we were not allowed to go with *him*. For maybe a month, I felt like I could breathe. We had friends buying us groceries and we were sleeping in the living room. It was the first time in years that we hadn't slept behind a closed, locked door. It was the first time in years I can remember my mom sleeping. It was very short lived. The turmoil was not very far away.

The nightmares and promised threats were all very close to coming true. I cannot say that our lives are not better with *him* out of it because they are. It is just the decisions that *he* made after *he* left that would lead to some of the hardest times in our lives. It would be the next two years when I would learn that life really is not fair. Life is not a fairy tale. Everyone who deserves to be punished is not. The justice system is not designed to help kids and that one human being can really ruin the lives of others. It would be the next two years when I

My Proclamation

would struggle daily with anxiety and panic attacks. When I watched my mom and siblings fall apart, and when I would learn who really loved us *and who really should never expect us to speak to them again. It would be these two* years that would make me question everything that I thought I knew.

The first visit came really fast. The week that led up to it caused so many tears from all of us. It caused many conversations from my mom about how *he* missed us and how *he* is working on *himself* and how things would be different. *he* was allowed to see us 12-6 on Saturdays. We all cried that first Saturday. I refused to get into the car. The other three got in with some hesitation, but I refused. My mom took me out on the porch with tears in her eyes and told me that it would be fine. I know I was really upsetting her because she was begging me to get into the car. She was telling me I had to go. She told me that she was going to be great because she was going to get lunch with Mrs. Wiscarver and her daughter, Lillian. She was the cheer coach at Orange High School and we had gotten to know her that summer because we went swimming with them and to lunch.

The second I agreed to get into that car and the door clicked, I knew my life was going to be different. I knew that I was going to be different. I just didn't know how yet. *he* talked about how *his* family was going to be there. I told *him* I didn't care because I didn't like any of them. I told *him* that they were all like *him* and hateful people. *he* picked up *his* phone and called them to tell them what I said even though we were about to see them. We met them all at a pumpkin patch. It ticked me off very much because my mom has always taken us to the pumpkin patch and *he* had always chosen to be absent. *he* bought everyone the biggest pumpkins and bought me one even though I didn't want one. *he* bought bags of peanuts and ate them right next to Scarlett. *he* tried to hold my hand and pull my hair. *his* family kept telling me how great *he* was and all the wonderful things *he* can do. Elaina and I wanted to do the corn maze. Instead *he* decided to take me in by myself and *he* stood there and screamed at me for not getting into *his* car and wasting *his* time.

When I tried to walk away, *he* would step over and block my path. *he* said I should never do it again, or else. *his* eyes were crazy, but *he* put this smile on *his* face. A smile that was not real and *he* said I love you so much. That one sentence made me sick. The rest of the day I watched the clock. I heard *his* family talk bad about my mom. *he* made comments about her in the car. *he* said she stole *his* money and had an affair. *he* said that she was a liar and not a good mom like *he* thought. These were comments that weren't true. *he* started talking about *himself* a lot. When we got back to my house, I couldn't get out of *his* car fast enough. I needed to get away from *him*. Away from the sound of *his* voice, the smell that smelled like our house that day, from the evil person I lived with for years, and from the guy who *he* was trying to be. I had to make it stop.

The next Saturday came extremely fast. There was no way I was getting into the car. It was this week that would be the beginning of my fight. It would be this day that I would put my foot down and say no more. It would be this day that I would never let him hurt me again, or so I thought. For months after months I had to go to the front door and tell *him* I wasn't going. I have stood face-to-face with *him* and have called *him* out on every single thing *he* has done. *he* stood there looking me in the face, telling me how crazy I am, how much help I needed. How *he* has never done anything to anyone. How all he tried to do was be a good dad but she made it not be able to happen. *he* talked badly about my mom every single time.

he threatened to call the cops and *he* said it would be very bad for her if I didn't get in the car. I have called *his* family out to their faces and have told *him* how much I don't like *his* mommy. Here's the thing, I did this every week knowing it was not making my mom happy. I did this every week even though I had this ache in my stomach and I was choosing to not listen

My Proclamation

to her. At first, Elaina and Scarlett would come home with stories of rock climbing and swimming. Eating out, candy, cake, etc. It didn't take long though for those stories to change. It is like vacation with *him*. *he* can only pretend for so long. I 100 percent back up my decision to refuse to see *him* and would support anyone else making this decision. It is important to note, though, that it would be the amazing people that would continue to pop up in my life that made it somehow work. If at any time one different person was replaced, this whole ordeal could have been completely different. As bad as my life is right now, I know that it could be much worse. I never take these people for granted and I never will.

It was sometime after Christmas when my mom mentioned the first life changing person to us. I was glad that Christmas was over. Elaina and Scarlett went for a sleepover at *his* house. It went horribly. Scarlett came home covered from head to toe in hives. Jack recently had his birthday party and had stitches in his chin due to falling in our car. *he* decided it would be a good idea to play football with him for the first time in his life and he came home bloody. Jack had refused to go the week before because they were going to go ice skating. I sat at the door for 30 minutes hashing it out with *him* that week. I told *him* how I saw what *he* did to my mom. I told *him* that *he* should just spend time with Elaina because she was *his* favorite. I even got Elaina and Scarlett to acknowledge that *he* had been spending every week bashing my mom.

The week before that was Jack's birthday and it took almost an hour to get him to go. The only reason why he did is because *he* bought him a drone and Jack really wanted to get it. *his* sister, Hillary, came into our house and tried to get him to walk out the door. She pretended like we were close and she had some interest in what was going on in my life. As time has gone on, I find this even more appalling because if anyone of them really cared, the next steps would not have happened. *his* family, every single one of them, are the same type of people as *him*. They want people to believe that they

41

are nice, caring people. In the end, they are all just full of themselves and cause so much pain. The only people they ever want to help are themselves. If they had any love at all for the four of us, they could have stepped in and told *him* to stop. Because unlike me, *he* usually listens to *his* daddy.

The days leading up to her arrival, my mom would discuss her with us a little bit. *he* had looked up her picture on *his* phone and showed Scarlett and Elaina what she looked like. They thought she was beautiful. My mom had already met with her and so she told us that we were going to love her. My mom had told us her job title, what her job was, and she told as that no matter how hard it was, we had to tell her the truth. The day that she came, Elaina and I were up in our rooms. Trusting people for us isn't always are strong suit. That is why when we find someone that we can, we attach ourselves to them and probably become annoying. My first thought to her walking into my room was that Elaina and Scarlett were right, she was beautiful.

My mom had gone to get the other kids. It is almost amusing, because Scarlett was really shy and hesitant. Now all she wants to do was see Caroline Cruz. She sat down on our bed and introduced herself to us. Her name was Caroline Cruz Nunez and she was our Guardian Ad Litem. She was wearing a long coat and I remember a lot of black. She repeated a lot of what my mom had said by explaining why she was there. She looked around our house and asked about our medals, who helped decorate our bedrooms, questions like that. It happened almost immediately, the feeling of knowing that she was going to be instrumental to us. I knew right away that I was going to like her and that some way she was going to be important to me. It would be over the course of a year and many months for me to really understand just how important. The bottom line is, though, Caroline Cruz was chosen to become our Guardian Ad Litem for a reason. Because of that, she would become so much more. The love I have for her is

My Proclamation

so great, it is hard to explain. It is hard to explain how you can love someone so much in just a short time.

I don't know if she knew at the time what an amazing thing that was and I don't know if she even today understands the true impact she has had on us all. She has helped me figure out who I am and what I want to be. She has helped enforce everything my mom has taught us by just truly being an amazing person. My mom was wrong. She said that we would really like her. That isn't what happened. We fell in love with her and she became our role model. She has become the first person I want to share my successes with and the first person I want to reach out to for help.

The next time we were to see her was supposed to be in February of 2018. Because I like to read and learn so much, I now understand why she had to ask us to complete the next step. I honestly didn't understand it at the time. My mom had to take us down to *his* house or rather *his* parents' house so she could visit with us with *him*. That whole week I had told my mom that I was not going to get into the car. I had shed a lot of tears that week. I know that the others were fine with it because where they were not excited to see <u>him</u>, it was another visit with her. The day of the scheduled appointment started off like any other. Throughout the day my body became so full of anxiety. I didn't understand what was happening then, but panic attacks were causing me to become un-kid like.

I was in class trying to type when all of a sudden, my fingers stopped working. I had this feeling in my head that was not right and my face started feeling numb. It was a terrifying feeling and I felt completely helpless and scared. I tried to ask for help but my words didn't come out like they should have. As I walked to the office, my legs felt like Jello or pudding. They felt completely disconnected from my body. That is the thing about trauma. People do not understand it, but it absolutely has one hundred percent control over your life. No matter how many times I tried to tell myself that the visit would be fine, my brain and body had a different plan. They were trying to tell everyone that I was crying out for help. They were trying to tell everyone what *he* had caused.

I think my mom called Caroline Cruz and let her know what happened, because my mom told me that Caroline Cruz would never yank me out of the car. She just needed me to get into the car to make sure that I was ok. Those two sentences were the only reason why I didn't become difficult at that time. It was this day after talking to her that I knew I could trust her. She didn't tie a rope around me, she didn't grab my arms and attempt to pull me. She came out of *his* house when we got there and climbed into my mom's car.

My mom stepped out of the car. She had tried to talk down my anxiety and had tried to get me to go. She would have had a better chance of getting world peace to happen. Caroline Cruz also said some things about how it would be okay because she was there. She always has this way of bringing you down when you feel like you are about to explode. She is really good at handling our moodiness. After our conversation, it was decided that I would stay in the car with my mom. I had fallen asleep during the car ride there and my body was still feeling odd. My mom had taken me to Target during their visit. She bought me a cake pop from Starbucks, a luxury that we weren't presented very often anymore. She drove around and sang at the top of her lungs, making me laugh and letting my body to relax. My mom was just like Caroline Cruz in that matter. She is the second and only other person that can help me when I get like that. My mom always finds a way to make things better.

The next couple months through school went fast like they usually do. *he* had tried to volunteer at the school, which was not going okay for Scarlett. I always found it rather amusing because *he* does not like people from India. *he* thinks that they smell and *he* would always complain about being a minority in this country. *he* also isn't very fond of kids, so *him* being there was all for show. I hope that everyone else knew that. Scarlett would come home every time *he* showed up and would beg my mom to make it stop. My mom would explain to her that *he* had every right to be there and if Scarlett was feeling scared or having some anxiety about it, then she would need to talk to her teacher about it and let her know. *he* also started dropping off letters for Mrs. Smith to give me. I have always found the way that she does her job isn't as great as others think. She doesn't have as good of an understanding about her students as she thinks she does. I have been bullied and name-called for years and her advice and intake on how the situation started and should go was always terrible. It goes back to the whole social media thing. Some people, even kids, are really good at showing you only what they want you to see. I have lived with a person like this my whole life. These girls at my school are mean, just like their moms. They are liars and fake. They like to pretend to be something they are not and sometimes they fool people. When she would hand me these letters, a little bit of the numbness would always return. I wish she would have thought out that plan a little better before she decided to make decisions regarding my mental health that did not do it any favors.

February 1st is Scarlett's birthday. With our birthdays being in the winter, most times they fall on days when we have to go to school. My mom had found a job working in our school district, helping a 5th grade girl. It was a job that I used to think she was made for. I remember sitting in class and hearing an ambulance sound. I was unaware of what was really happening in the office until later on that day. Here is the thing people need to understand. A child or adult really that has a severe peanut allergy can die. When your child is placed into a peanut free classroom it is for a reason. I am sorry that you might be so self-involved that you do not understand or care enough to for just one snack a day send your child with something that does not have peanuts in it. My sister gets hives and swollen eyes constantly at school because of people's ignorance. I promise you that Scarlett would trade places with anyone that wasn't allergic to nuts. I have watched her be tested for allergies twice now. She screams out in pain, a little too dramatic I will admit, but she doesn't like it.

Her own dad and *his* family, for someone reason, are so self-involved that it just doesn't make sense to them. Her allergy can kill her, and it will, if people don't stop being ignorant about it. A kid had brought in a jar of peanut butter for a snack. Scarlett started having a reaction to it at some point during the day. I don't know if it was on her hands and she just hadn't come in contact with it until recess, I don't really know that much about allergies as I do with the laws. I just know that it got to the point to where she was not breathing. My mom had been called and rushed down to the school to get her. They had to take an ambulance to the hospital because of it. Please do me a favor to try to understand. There are so many foods that your kid can pack for snack. You are really supposed to be packing a healthy snack anyway which should consist of a banana or carrots. As easy of a job it is to read a label for one minute, my mom has a harder job protecting my sister from you people. Please make better choices.

We had to start seeing a therapist. At first I thought that *he* had convinced Caroline Cruz and the courts that I really was crazy. I still don't really understand the purpose fully. Our first therapist's name was Dr. Dickson. I wasn't ever a fan of hers. It could go with me not really trusting people easily, but I found her to be rude and non-understanding. We also had to miss school every time we had to go see her. This completely ticked me off. Caroline Cruz came to one of our visits and that was cool. I had hoped that we would get to spend more time with her that day, but as my mom reminded us in the car, Caroline Cruz was working and has a job. Thankfully, these sessions at her office didn't last too long. I think she considered us being uncooperative and being rude or

My Proclamation

disrespectful, when really it was over the prospect of having to tell her what had happened. Trying to trust someone that talked nicely about my dad and not wanting to be alone with someone in a room ever again. I still have issues with that.

My mom has never been a gun person and neither are we. I don't like them, I don't want to see them and I don't want to ever shoot one. It was during one of their Saturday visits when something terrible happened. By now you are probably understanding that besides *him* being an abuser and antisocial (I have done the research and it does make sense), *he* is also a really bad decision maker and does not care about the safety of any of us.

Scarlett and Elaina were going through my grandma's house. This first part I have always found odd, but not surprising. I am sure *he* was sitting on the couch, engulfed in *his* phone, not pretending that *he* wanted to spend time with them. The girls decided to go through *his* drawers. I am unsure on what they were looking for, but they could have just been being nosey. It was then when Scarlett found a pistol. Elaina has shown me pictures of what it looks like. I have seen this gun in my nightmares many times. *he* has used it on Caroline Cruz, on my mom, and myself.

For some reason, Scarlett decided to not listen to any rules my mom had put in place about guns. The whole if you find a gun, you don't touch it. Instead, you tell an adult thing… I guess either way, *he* was the adult there so nothing would have happened. She pulled the gun out and held it in her hands. She found the bullets in the drawer below. It was then when *he* walked into the room. She turned around and pointed the gun right at *him*. She said that *he* stared at her with a smirk on *his* face. It was then when she decided to pull the trigger. That moment could have been a life changing moment. I know Scarlett had said that she wished there had been bullets in that gun so *he* would be dead.

The Middle

I fully understand where she is coming from and I, too, want *him* to disappear off this earth. Yet, pulling the trigger and actually killing someone is not the way to go. Knowing and watching that happen would have ruined her life. Scarlett is a very feisty kid but she also has a heart of gold. She would do anything for anyone. She couldn't have recovered from that. It wasn't until a week later when Scarlett sent my mom a picture of Elaina riding her bike and *him* going after her that the story came out. *he* had left Scarlett at *his* house, in a bad neighborhood, in a hot steamy car, by herself. *he* had left her there knowing she had found *his* gun. *he* had left her there not knowing what she would do next. *he* had left her there, not caring.

On top of the gun issue, the summer of 2018 turned out to be an eventful summer. I say this because a lot of things happened, but none of them were great. *he* had decided to take them fishing at some point. I can't remember the exact timing of this trip. I know *he* likes to think that *he* is a country boy and that is fine. We are city people and we don't like dead animals on our walls and I don't really like to fish. I don't judge people that do because that is their interest. I just find it boring. It is just not things we really like to do. Because *his* interests always trump ours, *he* decided on that day *he* could care less and *he* wanted to take them to *his* friend's fishing.

This day, like the day of the gun issue, could have turned out horrific and could have been life altering for my family. *hIs* bad judgment making led to *him* letting Elaina, who was twelve and really short and to be honest kinda spacey sometimes, drive *his* car around a pond with *him* inside of a house. *he* left my 6 year old brother at this pond who could have drowned by himself. Elaina drove the car around the pond and at one time almost went into it with the car. She then had an almost encounter with a tree that she didn't see because, lets be real, she couldn't barely see over the steering wheel. Then on the trip back to the house, she drove by my brother almost hitting him with the car because, yet again, she couldn't see him.

My Proclamation

When Elaina came home and told us about what happened that day, I couldn't believe it. I asked her about having integrity. I asked her why she would agree to do something so stupid. I know that she knows it is wrong and unsafe to do that. I think just during that second, she made a bad judgment call. She is most like *him* and she has those moments every once in a while.

My house was across the street from my school. Also across the street from the school, was a bunch of woods. There were many times when we would be outside playing that the hair would stand up on my arms because it felt like someone was in there. It felt like someone was watching. I used to think it was *him* and maybe sometimes it was. To this day I still do not like walking by those woods. My mom had run us to Meijer to pick up a few items. As we pulled up into our parking spot, my mom had received a text so she had taken a second to respond. A dark car had pulled up next to us, but this isn't a weird occurrence so no one paid any attention to it. There was an older man that got out of the car. As we started walking up towards the front of the store, the same man was standing by the entrance, staring at us. He seemed very odd, almost frightening. As we made it into the store, Scarlett started to stutter and started to try to explain something to my mom. She kept saying that she knew who that man was. My mom kept shopping and would almost dismiss her. She told her that she had never seen that man in her life.

That is when Scarlett informed my mom of a conversation, *he* had had with them a few months before. *he* had told them that *he* had someone watch us and they would send *him* pictures of us so *he* always knew what we were doing. She said that *he* told her that his name was Duke. Do you know those videos where a deer runs out in front of a car and its eyes get big and scared because it knows that it is about to be hit? That was almost the look on my mom's face. She instantly put down the item she was going to buy. She bent down very slowly to be at eye level with Scarlett and she asked her to repeat what she just said. Scarlett was able to tell my mom again more clearly than before. My mom thought about what Scarlett had said and then she told us that she is done with her shopping and we were going to go pay.

We got to the front of the store and do self-checkout. I know we didn't make it very far into the store so we must have had only a couple of things. As we were checking out, I saw my mom look up and she just stood there, staring. My gaze followed hers and Duke was standing at the window staring at us. We finished buying our stuff and got out of the store. My mom took a weird way home and I saw her looking in her mirror a lot. The whole time I wanted to get into my house, but she was like driving in circles and going a back route that is much slower. We finally got into our house and settled for the night. Our nerves, on the other hand, were not and it also would not be the last time Duke or anyone else would be watching.

During the summer months, we are always outside. My mom loves the sun and the heat and the outdoors. This day we had no friends over, so no one would know about this happening. We happened to look over to the woods. We were just jumping on our trampoline and our glance went that way. It was when we would see a man. He was wearing clothes that made him blend into the trees. He had what looked like a camera and was wearing glasses and a hat. I did not have my glasses on this day, so I was describing the first sighting using Scarlett's description since she has eyes like a hawk. Several days later was when I would be able to confirm what he looked like. It was completely frightening to know someone is watching you. We all ran inside and grabbed my mom. She came outside and when she got there, the guy is gone.

Many days after this day we would see him there. It got to be to the point where we really didn't want to go outside anymore. Staying inside and relaxing became a better idea. One day, my friend, Lincoln, was over. Our life and the things

My Proclamation

that have happened usually do not get discussed with many people. Of course, Caroline Cruz knows and so do our therapists. Some of my mom's friends know I am sure. But it isn't like us kids just go around telling everyone that *he* is an abuser. It is not something you want others to know, I promise you. Landon was jumping on the trampoline when he does what we did days before. His eyes just glanced in that direction and he also saw a man kneeling down in the woods, snapping pictures. Jack and Landon came and grabbed my mom. It was that minute though, that I knew I wasn't crazy. Here was someone that has no idea that this is going on and he also saw what we saw.

The last time I remember seeing this guy happened on a day where my mom was not having a good day. Just like the rest of us, she has many of those. Sometimes, life just gets to be too overwhelming. We were outside playing with my mom when she noticed him there. She didn't alert anyone, she just said that she needed to go to the bathroom really fast. She apparently was lying because she was only in the house for a few seconds when she came running out caring a baseball bat. The thing about my mom is this, she might pee her pants when she runs, but when she has to, she can still run very fast. She had flip flops on, which were not the right shoe for the sticks and thorns. She must not have noticed the scratches and pain until later. I could hear her screaming some not nice things as she was running in the woods. I just looked at the others and we all just laughed. Not that being watched is funny, but when my mom gets like that, it does become funny. She says the best insults and I really think that guy was lucky that she had the wrong shoes and he had a head start. She was ticked. I never saw his creepy eyes looking at us after that day.

Dr. Dickson was no longer going to be our therapist. I am not sure what happened, but my mom broke the news to us. We would be seeing a new therapist named Sharon. We were set for a four hour therapy session which included *him* and did not

51

include my mom. This would be just another decision that someone thought of that would not be in our best interest. This would become a theme of my parents' divorce. Let's see how much we can mess these kids up. Sadly, I feel like *he* was leading the parade. As the day came for us to attend this session, our opinions and nerves would not be able to be restricted. When the time came for us to leave, Scarlett slapped my mom in the face. As I saw my mom's nose start to bleed, I ran downstairs and out the back door. I didn't see the other two kids, but I would find out later that Elaina was hiding in the playroom.

One of us made a phone call to Caroline Cruz. If anyone was going to see the messed up situation, it had to be her. She was the voice of reason for us all. We ended up getting out of that session. I stood nose to nose with *him* for months on Saturdays telling *him* what *he* did. *he* called me crazy and told me I needed help every time. *his* lies were numerous. I will never waste another second of my life doing that. *he* tried to turn the story and make you believe *his* lies. Even though we got out of that particular session, we still had to go see her. Where I was glad that Dr. Dickson was gone, I hadn't expected it to get worse. When she walked out into the waiting room, my mom stood up to shake her hand and to introduce herself to her. She looked at my mom and said something like "I cannot talk to you until *he* signs a release." We all looked at my mom, needing direction. I could tell she wanted to say something and didn't really like what she said to her, but she saw us staring at her. She said, "Everything will be fine guys, go ahead and go back!" The only good news about this session going terrible and all four of us having zero nice things to say about her is that we would see Caroline Cruz very soon. Her job and the life of the kids she represents are always at the top of her list. Even though Sharon was not a favorite of us all, my mom would grow to like her as would I. It would become more the process that I didn't like and wouldn't allow myself to become part of it.

My Proclamation

The thing about the therapy process is this: I am one hundred percent sure it works. I am sure some people love doing it and really need it. When I give my opinion, it is just that, mine. I am not putting down people who go because I understand its importance. But I bet others will agree with me. When you are a kid and you are going through this process, all you do is talk about it. Everything that is normal is already gone and then any second you get to be a kid is taken away by talking about it. The court system brings in all these people. Well that one didn't work so let's try a different one. I feel like my family became like medical mice. They kept experimenting with us to see what would and what wouldn't fail. Sadly, they do not see and maybe do not care what turmoil that put us in. How changing a new therapist all the time is terrible. How forcing us in a room with a parent who has caused us trauma is not ok. The parent that has caused the trauma should be in some serious therapy. They should be the person being treated like a medical mystery. It will be this issue on top of many more that I will someday fight for change when I become an adult. It is us kids who have been put through this that need to rally together and demand no more. If others will not put a stop to it, then we must start putting our foot down.

Elaina and Scarlett were still going with *him* every weekend. They were starting to have some major issues every week with going and it took a lot of talking from my mom to get anyone to go. First off, Scarlett loves Caroline Cruz almost as much as my mom. We are pretty loyal people and Scarlett has people's backs. *he* started making comments to them about her. *he* told her that she had nice legs, *he* knew what color her house was, and that she lived on a hilltop. *he* knew that she was a democrat and what color car she drove. *he* knew that she had gay friends and she wasn't racist. *he* just knew too much. *he* told Scarlett that Caroline Cruz was a bitch and Scarlett did not mess around. She came right back and told *him* that *he* was.

53

he started taking pictures of them constantly. It got to the point where they started refusing to take them because *he* told them *he* wanted to show them to the judge. *he* started pulling their hair, like *he* had done to me years before. *he* was almost getting in car wrecks because Elaina said *he* was texting and driving way too much. *he* was causing Scarlett to still have reactions to peanuts and was bringing them home rather hungry because *he* refused to give her a vegetarian meal or because of all the crap *he* fed them. Elaina would spend every Saturday night in the bathroom, doubled over with severe cramps that would not stop coming. *he* had spit on a homeless man during one of Elaina's cheer competitions. It took over a year but we finally found this guy and Scarlett was able to apologize for what *he* did to him and we were able to provide him with a meal.

he had taken a black mask and put it on his face. *he* told Elaina and Scarlett that this was his Muslim mask and it is what they were to wear when they shoot Muslims. *he* told them that if they went out into the sun they would get skin cancer and die. *he* then took them to my Aunt Michelle's house and would not give them sunscreen to wear.

My mom took us to Chicago for a day. *he* found out about it somehow and *he* made them look up gun deaths and murders in Chicago. *he* told them that they would be shot and killed by the black murderers in Chicago. *he* told them that they don't just stay in those areas that they live, they come into the areas where we would be visiting. *he* told them to not go skating at Skate Zone because the black people go there and they would get shot. *he* then took them to Skate Zone. Everything out of *his* mouth was a way to make them experience fear. It was mean and it was the same way *he* parented us when *he* was there. Like the time *he* took the modem so we couldn't have TV at night. We didn't have cable in our room, we only had an Amazon fire stick. So for that one night, *he* got to pound on the door and kept us all up. That night *he* yelled that my mom will answer *his* questions until

My Proclamation

she learns to respect the man that feeds her. Jack looked up at my mom and asked her what was wrong with *him*. I wanted to tell *him* that I have been trying to figure that out for years.

By the time school rolled around, things were starting to calm down a little bit. We all got the teachers we wanted, we were able to get a few nice clothes for school. My mom got a new job at a Middle School in my school district. We were able to go to Zoombezi to swim for the summer and hang out with our friends many times. My sister was able to watch Brownie the rooster, her 2nd grade teacher's bird, who would tag along with us to the July 4th parade and other outings. I feel like this is also a part of our lives. As soon as things calm down, as soon as we get used to how life is going, it is like we are hit with another train. This next locomotive would be a big one.

The guy that owned our house decided to sell it. The home that holds all my memories - good and bad. The home that was my sanctuary. The home that lets us go to our schools was about to be taken away. I cannot even begin to explain to you how this made me feel. My stomach felt like something was inside and was just twisting and punching it. Every time a box was packed or a picture taken off the wall, it really hurt my heart. It was like this was the last piece of my life that I was trying to hold on to and it was now being taken away. The house search began. We would visit every apartment building and house that was for rent. We were told that we couldn't get a 2 bedroom house or apartment because our family was too big. We searched every night. You see, this whole event caused us so much anxiety. My mom has told us many times that people move every day and we would be fine and it will just be a new adventure. The thing is, when *he* constantly makes threats to you that you will one day be homeless, when your whole life is big one big "adventure", it gets to the point where you don't like taking trips anymore. You just want to stay put.

The Middle

Our search paid off, or so it seemed anyways. We found a house in our neighborhood to rent. It was such a nice house. It wasn't like my old house, but it was nice. We were all so relieved because it allowed us to all stay in our schools. All of my mom's friends and teachers from Liberty Tree came and helped us move. My grandma would come every day to take us to school because my mom had to be at work early. By this time, Elaina and Scarlett had stopped going to see *him*. On occasion we would still see Duke's car. The torment and stalking didn't stop there, though. We started getting knocks on our front door. Our furniture on our porch started being moved. Our dog Lucy, who is not a barker, started staring at the doors, barking for minutes. My nightmares became worse. They would be so graphic and they would usually involve *him* killing my mom and Caroline Cruz. They also usually involved guns, cars and hair pulling.

My therapist Sharon had recommended that I put foil on my windows, so we tried that. As dumb as it sounds, it did help me a little bit. It stopped me from feeling like I was being watched. It was a few months after we moved into our new house when some more amazing people would enter our life. For some reason we had to start doing visitations at the Visitation Center. It was going to be supervised visits with a police officer outside. There would be a few times when the feeling in my chest would come on our way to the place, but it would become a ritual that wasn't so bad. I say that probably because I never had any intention of going back and seeing *him*. I got in the car and traveled down there each Friday only to keep my mom out of trouble. There were also several workers there who would become almost like friends. Kevin, Claire, Heather, and the rest of the staff at the Visitation Center will never know how much they helped me and the rest of us during that process. This was another part of the experiment that the court put us through instead of fixing the problem - which is *him*.

My Proclamation

It wasn't long after we lived there that we started getting these notices on our door. They would basically say we had to leave the house within so many days. This meant one thing to me. On many of Elaina's trips with *him, he* would tell her a lot of things. *he* told her that my mom had an affair with a man named Zac Clemons. Earlier in the story I mentioned the Clemens family. I spend every moment with my mom and we sleep in the same room. I can promise you that never happened and it really upsets me that *he* thought *he* could say that. *he* also told her that *he* pays for us to have a house and if it wasn't for *him* my mom would be homeless. I don't know why *he* always likes to threaten us with that. It might seem like a dumb threat, but I can tell you that that threat would become really big very shortly. Because we were getting these notices on our door, I knew that meant *he* was not paying for our house. I knew that this meant that *he* was trying to follow through on *his* threat. We were put into a position like the one that we are in as I type this. We have nowhere to go and my mom never seems to have money.

We were able to stay in that house until after Christmas. I was able to celebrate my 11th birthday and have my friends come for a sleepover. We were able to have some important people over to meet Brownie during Thanksgiving. Christmas turned out great with lots of nice gifts, parties with friends and family, and we got to be all together. *he* didn't buy us gifts this Christmas which was great because I didn't accept anything from *him* the year before. When we got home from school on some day in January, I could tell that the time had come for us to leave. My mom looked very stressed out. She looked like she had been crying and there were totes everywhere. Not only did we have to move, we had to do it in 5 days and during a really bad ice storm.

Alexis was my mom's best friend. She is also my godmother. It was Alexis that we would call during times that were hard. When my mom was having an off day, we would call her to talk to my mom. We would have her come over and check on her. We have spent major holidays with her, spent the night at her house when *he* was going crazy, and it would be her who asked us to move in with her. She was always kinda fun to hang out with, similar to my mom in some ways, but only when her kids were not with her. Her daughter is ok. You could tell that she was treated like a baby by the voice that she uses and by the interests she has. You can also tell that she has never experienced the things that we have, which isn't a bad thing.

It is Alexis's son who is out of control. Anytime he would come over, he would break things. He would slap her in the face, spit at my mom, and completely destroy our house. He was out of control and he was never fun to be around and she seemed to have no problem with it. The only thought I had about moving in with him was that he also spent time with his dad and maybe we wouldn't be home with him that often. We also didn't have anywhere else to go, so beggars can't be choosers. Initially it wasn't so bad. We were all in school and we are always so busy that we wouldn't be home a lot at the same time.

As time went by it began to get worse. Alexis spent her whole day in her bed. She would be on her phone all day, laying there, spending no time with her kids. Noah and Natalie are completely on their own and are able to get away with making bad choices. Noah makes his own peanut butter sandwiches right by Scarlett, chasing her with a knife if my mom is at work. They eat Pop tarts 5-7 times a day and she does not cook for them. He pees in his pants and he makes everything smell like it because she doesn't change him. He also kicks, spits, hits, breaks things. He has kicked my brother in the head and the stomach. He has taken a stick to my mom's car, both sides and scratched it. On top of that, her dog is very mean. He has bit her kids a lot of times and so far has gotten Jack three times. This last time was on his leg and a scratch on his face and it was not good. Alexis would make us clean up after the destruction Noah had made. She would be upset when she would try to take a three hour nap during the day when we were there. Not that that is her problem but her kids are also there and he does not listen. It is really hard living with another person. It is not fun, and it is something I will never want to do again.

It is really hard to live with someone who is boring, who comes home drunk in front of us, and does not parent her own kids. I lived with *him* my whole life and now I am stuck living with someone just like *him* again. She talks to us just like *he* did. The big issue came when I decided one night to lock the deadbolt on her front door. See, here is the thing. Maybe a month before, notes were put on my mom's car. They told her to die and called her not so nice names. There have also been a couple issues with the dog barking and a knocking on our window. Alexis lives in a really old house and I am sometimes afraid that her door will not keep *him* out. That is why I lock the door like that every night. I am afraid that *he* will return. I am afraid that my dreams will come true. Alexis would become just another person who chose to take a roof over my head away. She would become another person who is clueless on how to treat kids, let alone kids who suffer from trauma like we do. Alexis is a guidance counselor in an elementary school, and I overheard her tell my mom she was doing the same thing to her students. One kid she started calling him all kinds of names. I don't need to say anything else about that, except maybe someone didn't find their calling.

My mom was at work when she started yelling my name. I heard how she screamed at Scarlett the night before and called her all the names that *he* had called us all before. I had been working on this Minecraft world for a week. Elaina had decided to give her kids my world for them to log into. Of course, as soon as Noah entered it, he destroyed everything I had built. Now I understand that that sounds dumb. But you have to understand that I am living in a basement, 30 minutes away from my friends, with my mom no longer home in the summer, and all of my stuff in a storage unit or left at our old house. I basically have nothing else to do.

I was upset that she did that so I went downstairs to cool off. I am unsure if this is part of my PTSD or just part of me, but I like to be by myself when I get angry so I can cool down. I need to think things through so I don't react in a bad way. I just need that time. I didn't like how she was screaming my name. She had not been nice to anyone since she woke up that morning and I was already in a bad mood. It is all my fault, because I didn't answer her at first. When she came downstairs she started screaming at me. She called me disrespectful. She called me a liar (which she has called us all now) and she called me rude. I felt like *he* was standing in front of me saying those things again. My chest started to hurt and I tried to tell her that I needed to be left alone. Some of it was because I was upset and I needed to calm down. The other part was because I didn't want her to see me have a panic attack. She screamed at me for 30 minutes. She refused to leave me alone.

My sister Scarlett, who likes to record everything, decided to record this. She then sent it along to my mom. I know my mom was busy working and I know we had all sent her a slew of texts that day complaining about how Alexis was being. The thing about Alexis is that she likes to tell her kids everything. I know this for a couple reasons. She started telling Elaina things and my mom had to ask her to stop. Also, on this day when my mom called, she put them on speaker for everyone to hear. Unfortunately for her, she screamed and yelled at my mom and my mom kept her cool. It was my mom trying to explain to her that we have PTSD and where she can understand her frustration, we aren't like our normal selves. Our feelings get hurt easier, we get triggered easily. Panic attacks come on sometimes for no reason. Alexis didn't get it. She said that she had never dealt with kids like us and all of our issues. That night my mom tried to talk to her about it again but it also got crazy. Alexis started screaming and

My Proclamation

losing it. It was then that she decided to come downstairs and tell us all that we have 7 days to leave her house or she will call the police. It was then that I dropped to the floor, blamed myself, and struggled to breathe.

The End

I have been searching for a new house. I know that my mom also has been searching for houses. We spend a lot of our free time driving around in Grandview and German Village looking at houses. We spend a lot of time driving around period. Being in this house has become suffocating, the same feeling as my first house. It has been really hard to live there since Alexis treated me that way. Alexis has taken Scarlett's shorts, told us we can't take showers, turned off the wifi. She has not been friendly and will not speak to my mom. I feel a lot of guilt over this. My mom sat down on the floor with me that night when she told us to get out and told me that it is not my fault. She said some people will never understand the struggles we have and some people will never be able to be empathetic towards others. She said that some people will never face adversity. She said that adults should not talk about things such as that in front of kids. I still feel really bad because I feel like I ended a relationship for my mom. But I also think that if she didn't care enough about us to treat us in a way that *he* did and not understand, I am glad she is gone. I am just facing again the possibility of being homeless. That scares me beyond belief. I just want to be a normal kid again, one who is given those basic needs. I don't know why that is too much to ask for. Time is running out and I am afraid of what will happen. I am afraid of having no options.

I used to be a more quiet kid. I never have liked people being upset with me and I would never stand up for myself. This divorce and *his* abuse has changed me. I have become stronger in some ways and weaker in others. I have also learned how important it is to have a voice and how important

My Proclamation

it is to stand up for truth and what it is right. It isn't easy by any means, but it is important.

During the process where we were getting the notices on our door, I started getting really fed up. I am still there actually. I am tired of being told that certain people who are supposed to be there to help us can't, because of their jobs or won't because they only pretend to care. I am getting tired of people just not doing their jobs. It got so bad that I started feeling like I needed to find someone to help us. Most everyone that is involved in our case just was not. I searched for many weeks. I made a list of attorneys and did some research and read their reviews. If they had a bad one, I crossed them off my list.

It was then that I found the one I had been searching for. I sent a letter to my guardian ad litem telling her of my plan. I then found this attorney's email address and sent her an email. I wanted her to know about my family. I wanted her to know about my mom and about *him* and about all the abuse. I let her know that I am a hard worker and I would do what I could to pay her back. I wanted someone to finally just care. I wanted someone to help us. I am not sure how much time went by, but this attorney emailed me back. She would become one of the most important people in my life. She would become a role model to me and I have never met her in person. My mom has and has told me that she is just as great in person. She has also become very important to my mom. Victoria Ryder decided to take my mom's case pro bono. She and her partner, David, were going to represent my mom. In that moment, I felt very strong. I felt like I really could change the world. I felt like my dreams really could be reached. I once told someone about a quote I heard on America's got talent. It had to do with how hard it is to dream when you are too busy trying to survive. That is how I feel about these last two years. Every time I felt like we would make it, a bus came and smacked me in the face. For a short period of time, Victoria Ryder gave me the strength to continue fighting. She made me feel like I could dream for a few days. It just became too

The End

much most days and exhaustion set in. It got tiring to always fight. It got tiring to work so hard and have nothing come from it.

A big opportunity came my way shortly after my mom met with Victoria Ryder. The possibility for me to maybe go to Columbus Academy was mentioned. I was able to go to the school and spend a day there. I met so many friends on that shadow day and I fell in love with the whole school. Their cafeteria is amazing. They have all of these choices, such as a pasta bar or a deli bar. All of the kids get iPads and they take swimming for a class. Their desks are on wheels and they are different colors. They got to watch baby birds be born and they do a lot of outdoor learning. In art class they were making guitars and I was able to make my own guitar pick. For that whole day I could see myself going to that school. I had to go take a test for them to see where I am with my learning. Everyone at that school had been so amazing to me and to my mom. My dream is to go to Harvard and kids who go there really do go to Harvard. Victoria Ryder is a human being that I don't get to meet very often. I know she had something to do with the opportunity. I believe when I first meet people that they are like her, but they show their true colors really fast. She has given my mom a job and has given me hope. Not really hope that I won't have to live in a bad environment or that *he* won't finally do what *he* always promised and kill my mom. She has given me hope that there really are good people out there. She had also proven to me that attorneys aren't what *he* thinks they are - at least not all of them. Victoria Ryder will always be someone I will work towards being like. I promise that I will one day change someone's life like she has changed mine.

I mentioned early on how *he* likes to attack people and make them live in fear. *he* is very good at it and *he* always gets away with it. Several months ago *he* texted my sister and told her to look at a sight on social media. It was an Ohio fathers movement page on Instagram. It sounded like an odd request but *he* had a reason for doing so. As soon as you log in, you see a picture of our guardian ad litem. You also see a bunch of memes and pictures about moms and how they are worthless. I had a really hard time with seeing this post. There are many reasons really. The things that are posted about Caroline Cruz are terrible.

I also have a problem with people sitting at a computer somewhere and bullying others. It is cyberbullying and it should not be tolerated. I tried messaging the owner of the page. I am pretty sure the site has some contact with *him* because how else would they get her picture? The guy was not the least bit friendly and at first tried to tell me I was not myself. I tried to explain how he had it all wrong, but this guy is just as crazy as *he* is and refused to listen. Later he would post a picture of another attorney named Julie Lawson. I know Caroline Cruz knows her and my mom would soon meet her. She is another attorney that just tries to help others and because of this becomes a target for others to go after.   In my opinion what this guy has done to Caroline Cruz and the other attorneys on that page is harassment. Shame on Instagram for not following their policy on this issue. One day I will stand up in front of congress and stand up for the Keely Lawson and Caroline Cruz Nunez of the world. Someday I will stand up to the court the way everyone has refused to do for me.

For almost a year I have had the plan of speaking to the judge in my parents' case. It has been promised to me by two people. I have spent hours thinking about what I would say. I have spent time in front of the mirror trying to figure out what I would wear. I knew that if I could just talk to her that I could make her see. I could make her understand. When I recently brought this up to my mom, she broke the news to me. She said that she and *he* were working to settle their case. She said that I probably wouldn't get the opportunity to speak to the judge and that was a good thing. When she was speaking to me, I really couldn't believe my ears. How can you settle with someone who only thinks of *himself*? The only reason why *he* would agree to settle is because *he* is benefitting in some way. I started researching. I found a lot of things online that I found baffling and frustrating. First, if a parent gets behind on child support, they can be put in jail. Yet, if a father makes his family lose their home and become homeless, no one bats an eye. People in the court system believe that two parents are better than one, no matter how mental or abusive the other parent is. These people clearly have never lived in a home like the one I come from and must have visited Disney World every year. Third, I have been told that it is always better to settle. I find this absolutely ridiculous. If there is enough evidence and a kid like me that is fired up for battle, why back down and take a settlement? There should be a winner and a loser at least in this case. I don't care if people say that I am just a kid so I don't understand. I can tell you that I am also getting very sick and tired of hearing that comment. I am a human being.

I am a kid and I might not have had the experience of living on my own and paying taxes. I have not gone to a poll and voted for a president, driven a car, or drank a beer, But I have been put through hell, had everything taken away from me, gone hungry, lost my house, my 2nd home and my school. I have had nightmares more times in two years than I bet adults have their whole life. I think the difference between these adults who keep trying to diminish me because of my age is that I am unafraid of standing up for what is right. I have fought evil and so far have won. Everyone else must be afraid of *him*. That is the only explanation on why they would back down.

During the journey of divorce, you will feel many feelings. You will feel angry, lost, confused and bitter. You will be lied to by people who claim to be on your side. You will lose friends and people and teachers who were so big in your life. You will literally be crying out for help for you and your mom and you will have people outright refuse to help you. You will text people and see that they are on Instagram but they will not respond to your texts.(Scarlett's trick and she feels let down,

My Proclamation

too) They will make deals with you, promises, tell you they love you, but ultimately they are just saying what they think you need and want to hear. If you look back, they are just repeated comments. Our life is their job. It is not their life. We are not their kids and they are not going hungry or left without a home. The justice system is set up to almost be cruel. I have called it child abuse several times. A parent can abuse their child and until there is rape or murder involved, everyone just does "their job" and no one pushes for reform. No one argues that what is happening is wrong. My life and the life of my family have become case numbers and another part of their schedule that requires emails.

As hard as this has been on me, I know it has been even harder on my mom. I have seen it affect her in every aspect of her life. She has lost weight, gained weight, stopped eating, started drinking, stop sleeping. Her hair is grey, her wrinkles more noticeable. Her arms and legs scarred as I am sure her heart and brain are as well. I have listened to her scream out in the middle of the night during one of the few nights she has been able to close her eyes. I have seen the fear and sadness - the light and pure happiness very rarely peeking through. I have witnessed her help others in ways they have no idea. I have seen her literally give her coat off her own back to a homeless child. I have seen her take clothes and give them to the same family because they have none. I have seen her cry real tears for others' struggles and losses. I have seen her give and care for people that would never do the same for her.

Divorce really does affect kids. So does living with an abusive parent. It does so more when you have a parent who cares less and lives their life to punish others. The system of the courts and attorneys is flawed and when I am able, I will do whatever I can to change it. I will complete law school and I will become a family attorney. I will become a guardian ad litem and I will be what I would hope they all started out as being, someone who wanted justice and wanted to help others someone who will stop at nothing to improve the lives of children.

As an adult, if you are in a bad relationship, you are able to leave it. Society applauds you for leaving. When you are a child stuck in this environment, society and the courts decide to force the relationship down your throat. Never truly understanding what long term effects it has on the child. When all the professionals try to determine what is happening with our families' dynamics, they need to start with this issue. I am that child, the one who would have kicked *him* to the road a long time ago, the child who they keeping choking from all the forcing. It doesn't matter if *he* is my dad because *his* treatment of me has never been considered by *him*. *he* never cared that I was *his* child.

Our words are very powerful. There were so many times that I prayed *he* would just hit me so the abuse would stop. Stop at least for that moment. The fear would go away after the hit until the next time *he* would raise *his* hand instead the pain of always lingering due to *him* opening his mouth. The words soak in. They have a very lasting effect on you. I have witnessed my mom and me both struggle daily due to *his* words. I have watched her be startled by a loud noise, scream at the top of her lungs with tears going down her face, gasp during her sleep. I have watched her change from being very sure of herself to someone who is afraid to make a mistake, someone who instead of facing the world head on now takes a back seat. My mom used to be the light at any party. She is the glue that holds us all together. *he* has taken so much from me that I won't let *him* take her too. She will get her light back. I will help her find the switch. We all need time to heal. Before you decide to attack someone, before that negative remark escapes your mouth, please stop and ask yourself if anyone really benefits from it. Will it really make you feel that much better to wreck someone's day? Why do you feel like you should dim someone's light?

My Proclamation

I am fed up with false promises. I am so tired of people saying they understand or that they are sorry. I am tired of people telling me they will help, but have no plans to. All kids want is to be loved, to feel safe, and to believe that the ones we love follow through with what they tell us. We want people to keep their word. If you won't be able to text later like you promised, then don't tell us you will. If you have no intention of helping, don't offer your help. Please stop coming into my life and getting my hopes up, just to let me down again. Please stop making false promises.

I have been told that the good guy wins in the end. My question then is this? Why does everyone allow it to continue? Why does the system not work as well as it should? Why does it take so long for anything to happen? Why do people claim to care but constantly make excuses why they can't help you? Taking action after a bad event happens is no action at all. It is cleaning up a mess. Remember that. Be the change you wish to see. Be the voice that won't go away.

My family needs help. We need someone to stop saying I am sorry and instead say I will help you. My mom has done so many things for so many people. I have been with her when she bought Christmas gifts, birthday gifts, anytime gifts for many. I have been with her when she purchased food for a family because a loved one was sick. I have seen her donate money to a cause and not put her name next to it. I have watched her cry over a loved one's pet that died. She bought a not so nice mom lunch for her birthday to "try" to teach us a point. My mom would do anything for anyone and not ask any questions. Where she is thoughtful and giving, she is also the funniest person I know. She danced with a drag queen at a baseball game. She sang some old song at the top of her lungs with an old man at Ikea. The thing is, though, my mom won't ask for help. She hides her suffering and her bad days. She will never tell anyone she is struggling. I have also seen this. She hides it, but not from me. I know!! I need just one person to help us. Help us find a house. Help us no longer be punished by *him*. I need someone to finally realize that *he* has been winning and decide to put their foot down.

he has abused my family for years. There are six types of abuse and *he* has committed almost all of them. *he* has thrown my dog down the stairs and into walls. *he* has tortured, terrorized, stalked, harassed, and embarrassed us. *he* has caused me to be hungry, caused me to lose my identity and question who I am and who I want to be. *he* has caused me to question if any guy is worth trusting and I do not like to be alone with anyone. *he* has taken every holiday and caused some anxiety. *he* has threatened my mom's life right in front of us, telling us that *he* was going to bury her ten feet under in some wooded area where no one will find her. *he* has given us huge knives to play with and has pointed them at my mom. *he* has tried to teach us hatred towards any other ethnic group. *he* has attempted to turn us into bullies like *him*. *he* has lied to the courts, to our guardian, to our therapists, and *he* is lying to *himself*. *he* is refusing to do things that will make my life better. *he* is refusing to do things that will help me succeed. *he* would say all the time that if any one of us got spanked or yelled at or demeaned in any way that every decision has a consequence. *he* has chosen to completely destroy my family. *his* consequence to this decision is that I will never stop until everyone knows what *he* has done. My voice will never go quiet................

I would like to be known as a person who is concerned about freedom and equality and justice and prosperity for all people.
Rosa Parks

The only tired I was, was tired of giving in.
Rosa Parks

Be sure you put your feet in the right place, then stand firm.
Abraham Lincoln

My Proclamation

There are still many causes worth sacrificing for, so much history yet to be made.
Michelle Obama

A winner is a dreamer who never gives up.
Nelson Mandela

May your choices reflect your hopes, not your fears.
Nelson Mandela